THE WORLD OF THE OLDER WOMAN

For
Carl Eisdorfer, Ph.D., M.D.
my unwitting mentor

THE WORLD OF THE OLDER WOMAN

Conflicts and Resolutions

Edited By

Gari Lesnoff-Caravaglia, Ph.D.

University of Massachusetts
Worcester, Massachusetts

Volume III, Frontiers in Aging Series
Series Editor: Gari Lesnoff-Caravaglia, Ph.D.

 **HUMAN SCIENCES PRESS, INC.**
72 FIFTH AVENUE
NEW YORK, N.Y. 10011

Copyright ©1984 by Human Sciences Press
72 Fifth Avenue, New York, New York 10011

All rights reserved. No part of this work may be reproduced or utilized in any form or by any means, electronic or mechanical, including photocopying, microfilm and recording, or by any information storage and retrieval system without permission in writing from the publisher.

Printed in the United States of America.
987654321

Library of Congress Cataloging in Publication Data

Main entry under title:
The World of the older woman.

(Frontiers in aging series; ISSN 0271-955X; v. 3)
Includes bibliographies and index.
Contents: Introduction/Gari Lesnoff-Caravaglia
Double stigmata/female and old/Gari Lesnoff-Caravaglia
The psychsocial problems of older women/Lillian E. Troll—[etc.]
1. Aged women—Social conditions—Adresses, essays, lectures.
I. Lesnoff-Caravaglia, Gari.   II. Series.
HQ1061.W67 1984   305.2′6   83-12958
ISBN 0-89885-089-4

CONTENTS

ACKNOWLEDGEMENTS

Some of the chapters in this volume are based upon presentations selected from the Annual Gerontology Institute of 1977 and 1979 held at Sangamon State University.

The Gerontology Institute is an annual cooperative effort developed by the Sangamon State University Gerontology Task Force whose membership includes agencies and organizations in the State of Illinois with interests in gerontology/geriatrics. The Task Force is chaired by the Director of the Illinois Department on Aging.

Co-sponsors of the Gerontology Institute 1977 and 1979 included the Illinois Department on Aging; the Illnois Office of Education; the Illinois Funeral Directors Association; the Illinois Health Care Association; the Order of the Golden Rule; Southern Illinois University School of Medicine; the Southern Illinois University at Carbondale Gerontology Council; and Roche Laboratories.

I want to thank Doris Westfall for the typing of this manuscript.

CONTRIBUTORS

Stefanie S. Auslander
  Interdisciplinary Doctoral
  Candidate
  University of Louisville
  Louisville, Kentucky

Adele Cooperband
  Quincey, Massachusetts

Wilma Scott Heide, R.N., Ph.D.
  Professor of Women's Studies and
  Public Affairs
  Sangamon State University
  Springfield, Illinois

Nancy Mayer Knapp
  Huntington Beach, California

Gari Lesnoff-Caravaglia, Ph.D.
  Executive Director,
  University Center on Aging
  University of Massachusetts
  Medical Center
  Worcester, Massachusetts

Paul S. Nathanson, J.D.
  Clinical Law Faculty
  University of New Mexico
  School of Law
  Albuquerque, N.M.

Eloise Rathbone-McCuan, Ph.D.
  Director Social Work Program
  University of Vermont
  Burlington, Vermont

Phyllis R. Silverman, Ph.D.
  M.G.H. Institute for Health
  Professions
  Massachusetts General Hospital
  Boston, Massachusetts

Marcia B. Steinhauer, Ph.D.
  Associate Professor
  Graduate Program in
  Administration,
  Rider College,
  Lawrenceville, New Jersey

Natalie P. Trager, M.S.W., Ph.D.
  Director, School of Social Work
  Grand Valley State Colleges
  Allendale, Michigan

Lillian E. Troll, Ph.D., Chairperson
  Department of Psychology
  Rutgers, The State University
  New Brunswick, New Jersey

INTRODUCTION

Money and the ability to amass it; the meeting of society's hopes and despairs; status which comes with social participation; control which is bound up in family life and parenting; education as the bridge to opportunity; sexual attractiveness which binds and lets go; the freedom of health—the lack of these is the signal of age.

When does a woman begin to realize that she is old?

When actions alter and behavior changes to a new accommodation of her, and there is the slow death of societal expectation.

When she begins to feel an erosion of her power grip on the world as what she has to say has little effect upon the listener—eyes shift and wander, and she is left without an audience.

When she is treated as part of the room's furnishings by men who turn their attention to younger—and often less attractive—women.

When reference to times gone by or less sophisticated days is made, and the comment is accompanied with an inclusive glance in her direction.

The determination of a woman of age to appear young is not born of vanity, but the knowledge that power lies in youth.

Should power reside in age, we might well find in vogue the trembling hand and shuffling gait, spectacles and hearing aid. The young feigning sensory loss and graying the hair or attempting its removal in an effort to appear venerable.

If the pace to be emulated is slow and measured, then the impatience and haste of youth is put to shame. When caution is preferred over imprudence, and deliberate action over trial and error, then youth is a lament and old age a herald.

When age is feared—not because of the proximity of death, but as the centrifugal force of life—then idolatry of youth will fade as will smoked glass and candlelight as fitting accoutrements for the woman of age.

Gari Lesnoff-Caravaglia

9

Chapter 1

DOUBLE STIGMATA
Female and Old

Gari Lesnoff-Caravaglia

Change that is the result of a graduated process in which persons are at least subliminally aware of its emergence, is change to which persons can adapt with minimal difficulty. Change which comes about insidiously and unexpectedly, brings shock in its wake and reverberations which persist throughout life. Many of the changes to which women are subject as they grow older have much of this second quality, and the life lived is often perceived as a form of betrayal.

The dominant response called for by society with respect to women is a biological one. A woman is schooled early in life to the fact that her role in society is a nurturing one—that of becoming a mother, and eventually a nurse to her aging husband who in most societies is older than she and will leave her a widow. Careers open to women were, and still are in large part, of a nurturant nature— teacher, social worker, or nurse. In the modern age we have not moved far from such restrictive aspirations for women.

While women have submissively played these culturally ascribed roles, it has not been until the middle half of the present century that women have come to the realization that such roles were only a form of manipulation. As larger and larger numbers of women continue to live beyond the period of fertility, the specter of lives lived in futility looms large on the horizon. Once the societal need was met, and the women was no longer regarded as *serviceable* or *productive,* society turned away in total indifference. It is this betrayal—the move from nurturer *par excellence* to feeling *de trop* or literally superfluous—that causes the feminine anguish of growing old.

The adaptation to the process of aging presents individual difficulties for which each woman develops her own coping strategy. It is the external context—society and its expectations—that exacerbates the problems inherent in such adaptation. The position of the post-menopausal woman who faces another near half century of life might well be paralleled to that of the biblical barren woman.

Much in the same way that Black persons cannot alter their color, and thus are conspicuous as a minority, the signs of age and the identification as female, even with the best disguises, really cannot be concealed. Women cannot change their sex—nor can the aged hide their wrinkles. These stigmata serve to keep the female—the older female in particular—from being absorbed into the mainstream of American society.

Women and the aged have shared with minority groups the experiences of subordination and frustration. They have not participated as equals in those opportunities which members of our society have grown to expect as part of the American way of life. (Barron, 1953) Many persons can live out their working lives without being affected by those factors which hamper the lives of women, Blacks, the foreign-born, or other minority groups. None, however, can escape the effects of age—male or female.

Of course, one can always cite instances of older persons being revered and regarded with respect. What we fail to notice, however, is that older people who earn our esteem are always older persons who personify other values which we treasure in about the same degree that we do youth. (Blau, 1973). Such older persons have either succeeded in business, in the arts, are reknowned scholars—or are simply rich.

To be noticed, an older woman has to be an exceptional individual. She must be something of the caliber of a Helena Rubenstein who, even into her nineties, was running an inordinately successful business. Or someone like Gloria Swanson who continued to be successful in two enterprises—the movie industry and the fashion industry—well into old age. Other examples include Susanne Langer, Hannah Arendt, Martha Graham, Georgia O'Keefe, and Helen Hayes who continued to be active on both stage and screen long past her seventieth birthday.

In the main, however, the attitude toward old persons is very much like racism. It is not surprising that the term that is often used is—agism. Agism simply means that old persons are frequently resented, devalued, forgotten, ignored, and even openly disliked. (Butler, 1975). Such discrimination, at times, is not deliberate or malicious, and makes its appearance through acts of omission. This does not render them less cruel, however. Examples may be found in the lack of adequate public transportation in areas where older persons live, or the use of vehicles which are not easily mounted by persons with ambulatory problems; or newspapers which refuse to print even one column in type large enough to be read by persons with visual difficulties, but which once a week issue an entire supplement devoted to the activities of teenagers. Still another, and perhaps even more significant example, is that of food manufacturers who do not package food in quantities suitable for one or two persons. Smaller packaging means a higher price. Since many older persons are generally buying only for themselves, they are not likely to be purchasing the giant economy size.

Another example of benign neglect is that of a group of older persons who stressed the need for better fire protection in residences for older persons and pressed for mandatory fire drills. They were told that such exercises were not needed, and that, furthermore, they would serve no purpose but to frighten the old people. Older persons are too disoriented, they were told, to profit from such instruction. And, besides, it was cruel to scare old people out of their wits with talk about fire.

The problems of older persons are not pressing concerns. The high cost of food is seldom seen in relation to the restricted resources of older persons on fixed incomes. One could well paraphrase the tale recounted of Marie Antoinette. When told that older persons can no longer afford the cereals which make up the diet of a significant number of them, those in charge of the public purse might well shrug and reply: "Let them eat meat."

The media has been far from helpful in destroying the stereotype of the older person. Several famous comedians regularly engage in imitations of older women, making them appear foolish and ridiculous. Sex jokes often deal with old men and impotence, or they are seen as "dirty old men." The older female is regarded as ugly and no longer sexually provocative. But it is interesting to note that there are no father-in-law jokes or stories that equal those which center around mothers-in-law.

Age discrimination, much like sex discrimination, is taught to children from their earliest years. Older persons are rarely pictured in children's books—outside of the visit to grandmother's farm on Thanksgiving. Parents of school-book children are always young. No one ever becomes ill. The only time the hospital is mentioned is perhaps when mother returns home with the new baby. Grandparents not only never sicken, they never die. One is certain that Dick, Jane, and Sally will remain the same bright, lovely children for ever and ever and ever.

On the other hand, children's stories and fairy tales are replete with old hags, harpies, evil crones, scary old witches, and mean old women of all sorts. No force is as cruel and evil as is the stepmother. Every child can imitate the "heh, heh!" of the old witch. Children also assimilate attitudes from the vocabularies taught them. They learn to use agist terms such as *senior citizens, oldsters, golden-agers,* and the like.

Agism is also reinforced by technology. There is an emphasis upon machines and production, new systems and new operations, and less and less emphasis upon people. Human beings become expendable. Just as there is a new model car every year to replace the present old one, so the habit of discarding and dismissing the old person is easily adopted. (Jacobs, 1979). Younger and newer are equivalents for better. Wives, particularly older ones, are seen as expendable in our society. This is only partly a reflection of the double sex standard. After all, what can a man expect once a woman reaches forty, but physical complaints, increased medical expense, a less attractive partner for social events. She might best be discarded for a newer model, in much the same way as you turn in your old car. Thus, we have become a throwaway culture in terms of people, as well as goods.

Although both men and women are victims of agism, the older woman is particularly devalued. Long before most women are physiologically dead, they experience multiple losses which cause them to shrink away as persons. (Curtin, 1972). The stereotype of the older woman is that that aging woman is not the equal of a younger woman—neither in power, nor in beauty, nor in any of the other feminine attributes. It is all right for a woman to be chronologically old, if she looks younger than her years. It is also all right for her to be sexual and old, if her skin and body give the illusion of youth. The emphasis in cosmetic advertising is always on looking younger than you are.

Few people realize the toll that such a devaluing process has upon women and their interpersonal relationships. Knowing that society, in general, harbors a negative view of the older woman, is it any wonder that older women hesitate to make new friends and often behave in a demanding or irritable fashion? Dressing up, making up, and dyeing your hair does little to bolster your self-esteem. The energy spent in the coverup detracts from the joy of existence and has an eroding effect upon human interaction. One of the most refreshing aspects of playing ''Let's Pretend'' is that it comes to an end at some point, and we then face reality. The old woman is caught up in the world of illusion and is offered no respite. This flagging self-image that needs constant buoying up has been one factor in the rising divorce rate among older couples. It certainly has been the cause of much marital disharmony.

What a woman learns, if she lives long enough, and women are doing so increasingly—is that her greatest value to society lies in her biological function of bearing children, and then, once held captive by this biological function, the burden of child rearing is her lot. She may prove useful, once her childbearing days are over, as a nurse for her husband as he ages. Since most women marry men who are several years older then they and that as a biological fact women live longer than men, she may well have this role to fill as well. But once women have accomplished these tasks, they can be dismissed as of no further value to society. That is, unless her adult children become disabled, and she must then repeat her nurturant role as parent.

The likelihood of living out one's life in a solitary state also calls for major changes in lifestyle which are caused by widowhood and divorce. The average age for widowhood in the United States is fifty-six, with two-thirds of all widows living alone. The number of older women who are divorced is growing. One in two American marriages ends in divorce, and at least one-sixth of all divorces are now occurring in the over-forty-five age group.

Also, as we move up the age scale, we find that the population includes more and more older women. The ratio at age eighty is close to 3 to 1 (Butler & Lewis, 1979) Thus, the possibility of remarriage for older women dwindles with age because of the preponderance of older women. For men, on the other hand, as they age, their choice of companions increases. Furthermore, older men can marry women, not only of their own age, but can choose much younger women—those in their twenties. If a women were to do the same, public censure and ridicule would soon extinguish any pleasure she may have found in the relationship.

Women in our society usually marry and have children. They are not accustomed to living alone. At the death of the husband, the women may find herself entirely alone for the first time in her life. Women find it extremely difficult to deal with their loneliness, and the prospect of illness is an ever-present specter. (de Beauvoir, 1972). Once they become ill, older women find little sympathy among physicians. They are usually not medically interesting cases. Their ailments are generally ascribed to "postmenopausal syndromes." And as they grow progressively older, they are labeled simply as "senile."

Living alone is a radical change in lifestyle for many women, but the difficulties of single life are compounded by the fact that in our society women have been led to believe that they require a man to fulfill their existences. Since older men are hard to find, old women seek out substitutes. Sometimes the substitute is God. At least he is a male-like figure to whom she can turn. Unfortunately, the benefits of religion are lost to such women, because religion rather than enhancing their lives, becomes a substitute for living. An example is that of older women who attend church several times a day, or who become vocal fanatics on the subject of religion. At other times, the substitute may be a nephew or grandson, on whom the aging female "dotes." A less rewarding substitute is that of denying her own aging, and making futile efforts to become a "swinger" and hope thus to retrieve the lost interest and admiration of men.

When we consider why many women have married in the first place, we find that marriage came about because of family pressure or societal expectation. By the simple lack of opportunity to select a more compatible lifestyle, women were co-opted into marriage.

There is nothing we associate with the word *bachelor* which is particularly demeaning or derogatory. Rather, bachelor connotes something of freedom, a sexually fulfilled life, or at least a life full of many kinds of social opportunities. Certainly *bachelor* does not equate with *old maid*—(although if a man is not considered sufficiently masculine, he may be dubbed an *old maid*). Thus, anything was preferable to the label of "old maid," even though many women may have preferred to lead single lives. This is an excellent argument for supporting educational programs designed to provide older women with opportunities for late-life careers. This is one way to compensate a past inequity.

It took Alvin Toffler an entire book, *Future Shock,* to describe today's world, while the former Nikita Khrushchev summed it up in a few words. We have gone in one generation from the outhouse—to outer space. Women cannot take advantage of such a sudden transition because they are not prepared for it. Such a technological "leap" can only be made by persons who have been active participants in the world, and women have been passive observers.

The problems of old age in the industrialized world are largely the problems of older women. The entire industrialized world is growing older, but within these populations, women are living longer than men. Women in the sixty-five and older group are the fastest-growing segment of the population. In the United States, it is these women who are the single poorest group within the nation's population.

Except for the affluent minority, most women will, under present conditions, become poor if they live long enough. In the United States, the official poverty rate for elderly women is 60 percent higher than for elderly men. Women's longevity also makes them more vulnerable to inflation. Since almost half of the women in the United States work without pay in the home, women are likely to face poverty in their retirement years. Women receive less in Social Security benefits because they receive disproportionately lower wages, often in part-time jobs, or in careers which are discontinuous because of time taken out for homemaking and childbearing. (Moss,

1970) When a woman's contribution to society is calculated to determine her Social Security benefits, a zero is averaged in for the years she spent at home in a career which was socially designated and approved.

The longer life accorded woman calls for a further adaptation, and that is to a life which includes illness. New diseases arise against a background of pre-existing diseases and disabilities, but also of a slow decline in the functional capacity of most body systems resulting from physiological or nonpathological age changes. Whereas the younger patient has but a single diagnosis, multiple diagnoses are usual in older women.

Prescription-drug abuse is a problem for all ages, but it is especially so for older women who use these drugs out of proportion to their numbers. Particularly disconcerting with respect to drug over-use is the fact that the wrong drug or the wrong dosage is frequently prescribed.

A further adaptation calls for a more restrictive lifestyle for older women who live in urban areas. Older women are most likely to be victims of burglary or mugging. There is an increasing incidence of rape of women in their eighties and older. Many older women die shortly after falling victim to criminals because they could not live with the feelings of fear and shock which the attack precipitated.

The prospect of concluding one's life within the walls of an institution is frequently an experience of older women which calls for major adaptation and reorientation of self-image. Three-fourths of all nursing home residents are women.

An even graver disadvantage haunts the late life of the female. There is increasing evidence that prolonged confinement in an institution, regardless of how genial the setting, is conducive to mental and physical deterioration. An institution simply is an artificial setting. In much the same way that correctional institutions are not "homes" or "schools" for children, nursing homes and retirement homes are not the "real world" for its clients. Separation and isolation lead to deterioration that is far greater than would have occurred had the person remained in his own home or within the community. These alternatives are open only to women of some means.

Although most older persons live in their own homes or with relatives, there are supposedly a little over one million older persons in institutional settings. Such residents are, by and large, women. This is a further indication that older women, who do have a longer life span than males, are unable financially to maintain an independent existence. This situation is caused by limited access to employment opportunities and educational advancement, as well as lower earning power. Realistic salary scales and benefits would offset this imbalance.

The biological betrayal thus is not only a limitation in terms of role possibilities for a woman, but her entire mental framework has been geared to activities within a restricted sphere. Once the family unit is dissolved, either by children leaving home (resulting according to some researchers in the empty-nest syndrome), or the death of the spouse, or by divorce, the woman finds herself in a situation not unlike that of being suddenly transported to a foreign country. The lifestyle offered her bears no resemblance to the life she has lived or has been conditioned to expect to live. Society is suddenly reflecting a new image of her delimited by the uncharitable perspectives of agism and sexism. She must adapt to a new social climate that is no longer made up of the intimate family circle. She must learn to cultivate new skills to promote her independence. She is expected to make important decisions with regard to her life without ever having had much experience in individual decision-making. She needs to use a currency which is totally foreign to her in that family finances were often not her responsibility. She must adapt to a new language—a new idiom—which was never part of her restricted vocabulary.

While circumstances which surround the older woman of today may significantly alter in future generations, there still persists an anachronistic orientation of women to their real possibilities in the world. Women have yet to be educated to the simple fact of their increased life expectancy. We may have moved a bit beyond the notion that to keep a woman in her place meant keeping her barefoot and pregnant, but we have yet to encourage women to begin planning to live to reach advanced ages with primary reliance upon themselves. Such a fostering of independence among women is one of the main challenges facing contemporary society.

REFERENCES

Barron, M.L. Minority Group Characteristics of the Aged in American Society. Paper presented at the Second Institute on Aging, Washington University, St. Louis, Missouri, April 17–18, 1953.

Blau, Z. *Old Age in a Changing Society.* New York: New Viewpoints, 1973.

Butler, R.N. *Why Survive? Being Old in America,* New York: Harper & Row, 1975.

Butler, R.N., & Lewis, M.I. *Aging and Mental Health,* Saint Louis: C.V. Mosby Company, 1977.

Curtin, S. *Nobody Ever Died of Old Age:* Boston: Little, Brown and Company, 1972.

de Beauvoir, S. *The Coming of Age.* New York: Putnam, 1972.

Double Jeopardy... The Older Negro in America Today. Publication of the National Urban League, New York, 1964.

Jacobs, R.H. *Life After Youth.* Boston: Beacon Press, 1979.

Lopata, H.Z. *Widowhood in an American City.* Cambridge: Schenkman, 1973.

Moss, Z. It Hurts to be Alive and Obsolete, or, The Aging Woman. In *Sisterhood Is Powerful,* Robin Morgan, Ed. New York: Vintage Books, 1970.

Occasional Papers in Gerontology, No. 11, *No Longer Young: The Older Woman in America.* The Institute of Gerontology, The University of Michigan—Wayne State University.

Chapter 2

THE PSYCHO-SOCIAL PROBLEMS OF
OLDER WOMEN

Lillian E. Troll

NORMS AND BIASES

Somewhere near the beginning of the women's consciousness-raising movement, in the early 1970s, I was invited to give a talk about women, and wrote a paper called "I Am A Woman. Who Am I?" That paper wrote itself and clearly came from my heart. Its major theme was that, as women, we are just not important. A young woman has much greater status if she dates the high-school senior class president than if she is herself elected president. Physicians in Russia, where 60 percent of doctors are women, have much lower status than do physicians in countries like ours where they are mostly men. The way to upgrade the status and pay of an occupation is to encourage men to move into it—and vice versa.

Furthermore, like all social norms and stereotypes, this basic sex difference in status is so ingrained in us that even though I thought of

21

myself as a feminist, and was raised by an early avowed feminist, I still had different expectations for my daughters than I did for my son. Our sex bias is rooted deep within us. Any consideration of older women must include two kinds of stereotypes, those dealing with sex and those dealing with age—both powerful as well as intertwined. Our rating of ourselves as good or bad depends on whether we believe we are on time in our developmental behavior, and these age norms are different despite our sexual revolution, despite the woman's movement, despite everything, for men and for women.

My second consciousness-raising experience was when I was asked to speak by a NOW chapter. I called that paper "Poor, Dumb, and Ugly," and considered the plight of the older woman. Again the paper wrote itself and provided me with a number of new insights. Incidentally, I made the mistake of including these two papers in my *vitae* and thus took an extra year to be awarded faculty tenure. My male faculty associates said, "Look, she's not really a serious psychologist; she writes about trivial, unscholarly subjects like women."

My third reaction to the woman situation derives from an experience I had recently, in fact, just a week ago. I went to a meeting of a group of older women on campus. When I walked in and looked around, I said to myself, "This is a batch of old women," and thought, "Why am I included with them?" I knew, of course, that I was an older woman myself, but...They were fat; they were sort of slouched; they looked poor, dumb, and ugly. That couldn't be me! I still feel this way when I see my picture in a newspaper. Candid shots are not for us. All of the reactions which I deplore in others, I realize, I also share.

There are, I believe, three kinds of bias. The first kind is expectation—what we believe a man at a particular age should be like—and what we believe a woman of that age should be like. This is true for all phases of the lifespan. Children are supposed to act like children, little girls or little boys, and we get very upset if they don't act appropriately for their age and sex. Adolescents are supposed to act like appropriate-sexed adolescents. Middle-aged men and women are expected to act like middle-aged men and women. These expectations are so strong that when we meet somebody who does not fit our stereotype, we distort what we are seeing, what we are hearing, what the person is saying or is really like, in order to fit. In that meeting with the other older women, after I'd been there for an hour, I saw how much I had been distorting. When they started to talk, they turned out to be sophisticated, interesting, witty persons. When I first walked in I had been wearing my expectation glasses. It was not comfortable to realize that I probably looked as uninteresting to them as they to me. They were all looking around uneasily, and no doubt feeling as dismayed as I.

Aside from expectations and their corollary distortions, there is a second aspect of bias, restrictiveness. There are certain ages when people *have* to do some things and *must not* do others, all depending on their sex, of course. Probably the most restrictive age is early adulthood. You really *must* do certain things when you're a young adult. Your parents, for instance, are ashamed if you do not at the proper time, enter into marriage, particularly if you are a woman; secure an occupation, particularly if you are a man; or have a child or two, in both cases. There's a lot less restrictiveness in later life. Let's hang on to that one positive thing.

The third kind of bias has to do with agism or sexism—negative attitudes. Such views target women in general and are most evident toward old age. We have an entire set of negative attitudes toward old people which make those who are older feel declassed, and those who are younger feel uneasy about associating with such inconsequential individuals, or about getting old themselves.

A friend who had been a pioneer in the woman's movement said that one of the first advantages that came out of the woman's movement was that women could now have women for friends. At first her comment startled me. Then, as I reflected, I realized how unaware I was of my own feelings about the undesirability of having women for friends. It was always accepted that women should cancel appointments with other women when they received a conflicting invitation from a man. Any activity which involved only women was of lower priority and carried less status.

This same kind of negative attitude exists with regard to old men, but it is magnified when it comes to older women. To have an old woman for a friend is nothing. When Sandra Candy (1977) investigated the functions of friendship in men and women of different ages from high school students through retirees, she found that intimacy-assistance or self-disclosure and helping was the most important function, almost serving as the definition of a friend. Unless you could really share your secrets, this was not a friend.

However, what is more relevant here, the second most important function of friendship was status, that you got something out of being known as this person's friend. This function of friendship was not constant in importance throughout the age span. It was most salient among adolescents, but gradually less so through the adult years. In the oldest group, post-retirement, the importance of status rose again, almost equalling intimacy. If status is so important in old age, you would want friends who would make you more important, and you could feel demeaned if the only friends you could find were other old women.

POOR, DUMB, AND UGLY

Old women are perceived by themselves, as well as by everybody else, as poor, dumb, and ugly. How valid is this perception?

First, are they poor? Well, most people over the age of sixty-five are poorer than other age ranges in the population, and most people over the age of sixty-five are women. On the average, one could say that indeed older women are much poorer than anybody else. They cannot go out and buy themselves new clothes with any frequency, even if they could find some that would look well on them. Of course, there are some very rich old women who can afford face lifts every 5 years, and good medical care, but the great majority *are* poor.

How about dumb? The amount of formal schooling in the American population is proportional to age, with each younger generation having more than its parents. In my research of 200 three-generation families, grandparents, their children, and their grandchildren, all adults, only a handful of either the grandmothers or the grandfathers had any kind of college education, counting as college everything like business school, dancing training, or nursing. Most of the oldest generation had just a few years of school. One-fourth of their daughters had some college, and one-half of their granddaughters. Across the country, we have experienced a steadily increasing level of educational attainment for both sexes, but most notably for women.

What does education do? In my three-generation study, the youngest generation, the granddaughters, were much more cognitively complex than their mothers and grandmothers. They saw life from a variety of perspectives, not only their own point of view. They also tended to have more of a sense that they could control their life and their world—a more internal locus of control. They also had higher achievement motivation. The oldest generation, those women who are old today, have had much less schooling than their granddaughters or their daughters. Therefore, when we say dumb, we are thinking relatively, relative to younger and better-educated generations. Of course, there are many women of this oldest generation who are far from dumb, far from uneducated.

The third descriptive term is ugly. We do not generally recognize, I think, the significance of appearance, particularly for women. A study by another of my students (Nowak, 1976) looked at this effect among men and women of three generations—young adults, middle-aged, and old. Using photographs of these three age groups made up to be either attractive, plain, or unattractive, she found that middle-aged women had great difficulty differentiating between youthfulness and attractiveness. None of the men had this problem, and neither did the young or the old women. Middle-aged women were uniquely sensitive to appearance. They judged the "attractive" pictures as much younger than they were and when told a woman was 10 years older than her actual age, they considered her unattractive. The photographer reported, also, that he had difficulty with middle-aged women models, who refused to be "made up" to look unattractive.

It appears that until we can change our attitudes about attractiveness, older women are going to feel unhappy about their looks. Built into our societal outlook is the idea that old is ugly.

Originally I thought that poor, dumb, and ugly was a sufficient description of the older woman. Now I feel there is an additional adjective: older women are unimportant. Young women are getting more important than they used to be years ago, but old women remain low in status.

•   •   •

FAMILY

Within the family there seems to be a different kind of emphasis upon older women. We look at our parents in a way that is quite different from the way we look at other people of their generation. Dr. Vern Bengtson at the Andrus Gerontology Center of the Universtiy of Southern California has reported his extensive research on generational perceptions. In a review of his work as well as of others on the topic of generations in the family (Troll & Bengtson, 1979), he and I conclude that family generational relations are closer than most writers have led us to believe. For instance, the rebellious youth of the last decade were not rebelling against their parents. They might say many negative things about older people in general but, "My parents are different." Parent-child bonds seems to continue practically throughout life. The only adolescents who really hate their parents, and the only parents who hate their adolescents, are those where there has been a long history of disturbed family relationships.

On the whole, most older women when they're asked about the empty nest, will say, "What empty nest?" First of all, they'll say they can hardly wait for the children to leave and then, a couple of years later, they will say, "When *are* they going to leave?" Their children, it is true, went off to college, or they went off and got an apartment for themselves. And yet, every single closet in the parents' house is full of their clothes and their toys. They come home as often as they can to get their laundry done or to catch as many meals a week as they can. That's the easy part. The hard part is that they come home with all of their problems too. Once they get married, and particularly once they have a child, there they are right back in intimate contact with their parents (Hill et al., 1970).

Therefore, the older woman is poor, dumb, ugly, and unimportant, but not necessarily in her own family. The aging of a mother is a heartache. Her children may be misguided in their actions, but most of them—and this has shown up in almost all survey data—take on the care of their parents longer than they should, either for their parents' sake or for their own. Most care provided for older parents who need it is provided by spouse or children (Troll, Miller, & Atchley, 1978). Many times, children of ailing parents don't take them to the doctor when they should, in part because of our common expectations that old age is illness. The old people complain of aches and pains, but say, "After all, I'm old." Unfortunately, doctors can also say, "What do you expect at your age?" Instead of treating older patients as they would younger patients, doctors too are influenced by our common age biases. The same holds for psychologists and psychiatrists.

Surveys of old people found that 80 percent of all people over sixty-five had at least one child (Troll, Miller & Atchley, 1978). Of those 80 percent who did have children, over 90 percent had seen at least one child at least once during the last week. They lived within a half-hour walking distance, or within a half-hour approaching distance. If they were poor, it was walking; they tended to live in the same block. If they were rich, it might be further away, but they kept in touch by more expensive means, cars, trains, planes. There was a constant exchange of services and help. No matter what happened—if the children got richer or poorer, went up or down the social scale, ties with parents remained. This kind of deep-seated bond takes years to build, and is not easily destroyed. Parents and children do not have to share attitudes or values, don't have to live nearby, don't even have to really like each other. No matter what, they continue to see each other, stay in touch, and continue to care. The feelings of parents are probably quite different from the feeling of their children. Parents remain parents and children remain children. All throughout life, when parents are asked about their children, they refer to them as *family*. Their children, though, use words like *relatives,* a more distant kind of term. Relations with friends highlight the special kinds of ties among family members—particularly husband and wife and parent and child. Friends are for fun, usually; family for obligation and commitment. People are more likely to change friends than parents.

DISENGAGEMENT THEORY

Throughout the latter part of the 1950s, and the greater part of the 1960s, disengagement theory held center stage in the gerontological field. It evolved from the early findings in the Kansas City studies on aging conducted by a team from the University of Chicago. In 1960, Cummings and Henry published the first results from that study in *Growing Old.* It included the two-part disengagement theory. The first part, abundantly replicated since, stated that as you got older, you withdrew more and more from society in tune with the withdrawal of society from you. Activity theory, which had predominated earlier, assumed that society rejected and dehumanized older people and that the inclusion of old people in ongoing life events would reverse a good deal of the observed decrements of aging. If children or others weren't so neglectful and rejecting, said activity theorists, then older people could remain integrated within society, and continue to enjoy life. The stress on mutuality of withdrawal by disengagement theory relieved many guilt feelings.

The second part of disengagement theory offered an explanation of the observed decrements in involvement by older people in the world around them. Cummings and Henry suggested that these were preparations for death, a ''natural'' process. Therefore, they predicted that if you measured the morale of older people. you would find that those who disengaged the most, who withdrew most from the world, would be the happiest; they would be doing what nature intended them to do. Later analysis showed, however, that those who disengaged the *least,* who stayed most involved, had the *highest* morale. More recent research points to a more complex picture, with personality and life style showing up as the most important predictors of both extent of disengagement and morale. Thus, people who were always highly involved, are likely to remain so, and if involvement had always been good for them, they would continue to have high morale. More passive individuals could withdraw and be very comfortable with their reclusive existence.

Social policy based on an assumption that everyone reacts to the process of aging in the same way is misguided and doomed to failure. For instance, trying to get all old people busy would make the rocking-chair people miserable. Trying to get all old people disengaged will frustrate the engagers. Policy has to consider past behavior.

But policy also has to consider the effects of the age biases we discussed earlier. Lowenthal et al. (1975) found that those personality characteristics that were associated with happiness in men in their forties and fifties were associated with anxiety and discomfort in men ten or so years older. Dynamic, aggressive middle-aged men are rewarded. Dynamic, aggressive older men are not. Obviously, our data present a challenge. Engaged people show signs of stress in their sixties, maybe, but still end up having higher morale than the disengaged.

We need to know far more about personality in the later years before we can speak with confidence about life-style covariants. We may be dealing not only with individual life-style variations, but also with geographic and subcultural variations. When I attended the International Gerontological Conference in Russia in 1972, I was struck by the difference in orientation between the eastern and western countries. Scientists from the western countries were concentrating on ways to improve the morale and life satisfaction of their older citizens. The people in the eastern bloc were interested in keeping their people alive and working and contributing to society as long as possible. Every single older person was needed, and the papers of eastern scientists on exercise and nutrition instead of residential and recreational activities reflected this perspective.

Older people do not disengage *from* the family; rather they tend to disengage *into* the family. Golden wedding couples, who are the elite of the older generations in more than one way, are usually closely knit and highly involved with each other (Parron, 1979). They are also closely tied to their children, particularly the women, but not as close as to their spouse. These couples are the survivors of their cohort, not only as individuals but even more as couples. It is true they are not as prone to divorce as younger couples. When they were young, they needed each other for survival. The women needed their husbands for economic support; the men needed their wives as housekeepers and companions. They also believed being married was important enough to make sacrifices for. Aside from usefulness, though, they admitted that marriage was something they'd had to work at.

Research on marital satisfaction (Troll, 1971) shows it to be highest in the first few months and years after marriage. It goes steadily downhill afterwards. Divorce statistics underline this decline. The greatest incidence, or the greatest frequency of separation and divorce, is in the first few days and weeks of marriage. Thus the lower degree of life satisfaction of couples that stay married for ten or twenty years excludes those couples that have already split up.

The divorce rate has risen for all ages, but the age profile has not changed. There are more divorces in the middle and later years of marriage, but the highest rate is still in the beginning of marriage.

The birth of the first child is a major crisis in life, particularly for women. No matter what their ideology about sex roles and sharing of family tasks, new mothers move into primary responsibility for children while their husbands shift their focus and time to their jobs. Many new mothers come to sound very stereotypically feminine indeed.

We still do not know much about marital satisfaction after the children leave home, in the post-childrearing family. Some studies find that it increases at this time, but other studies do not find any change (Troll, Miller and Atchley, 1978). Is there a post-childrearing second honeymoon? If there is, it is likely to be associated with a marked change in interaction style. Young couples tend to have very "hot" relationships. They fight a lot; they make love a lot; they go out a lot together; they talk about themselves to each other; they talk about their parents a lot; and when they have small children, they talk about their children a lot. They're heavily involved with each other (Feldman, 1964).

Twenty or thirty years later, they talk about what is going to happen in China, or whether it is time to put up the storm windows. They don't have as many fights, but they don't have as much fun, either. Their sex is stale. Their relationship has "cooled down." We could postulate an attraction-attachment polarity. Newly formed couples are attracted to each other while long-married couples are attached to each other. They may have equal scores on marital satisfaction, but they are satisfied for different reasons.

It seems that as humans, novelty is important to us. Something new is exciting; it is attractive. But we have no deep attachment to it. If a recently formed couple separates, mourning is not as profound as if a long-standing relationship is terminated. On the one hand, "there are many more fish in the sea." On the other hand, there is a feeling of great loss, even if the attached person—or object—was more a burden or irritant than a delight. Many people who turn from old attachments to new attractions are surprised when they find themselves upset. Pathological physical as well as psychological symptoms occur at the time of divorce or the death of a parent—even if they had little to say to each other for years. This is, of course, particularly true for widowhood.

There are more and more single women with each decade of life. Few of these, though, are women who have never been married. In this country, a very small percentage of people have never gotten married, something less than 5 percent (Troll, Miller, and Atchley, 1978). Jessie Bernard (1973), correlating mental health data with marital status, concluded that marriage was good for men and bad for women. Married men are much better off than single men in any index you can name. Single women, however, are better off in any index you can name than are married women. Bernard quips that men who never marry are at the "bottom of the barrel;" while women who never marry are the "cream of the crop." One explanation is that superior women did not have to get married.

As we go up the age scale, we find that there are more and more single women. This group is composed largely of women who have been married. About 95 percent of American women living today have been married at some point in their lives. There are enormous sex differences in the percentage of people currently married. When you reach the eighth decade, approximately 36 percent of men are married and only 6 percent of women.

McKain (1969) studied remarriage in old age, interviewing 100 couples with at least one member over fifty-five who applied for marriage licenses in Connecticut. Remarried men had been widowed for 32 years, while remarried women, on the average, had been widowed for 7 years. These couples tended to marry somebody they'd known most of their life. Most of them were happy, particularly if they had married for love, if they had their own home, and if their children approved of their marriage. It is interesting that marriages of young adults fare better if their parents approve, marriages of old adults, if their children approve. The family is central.

Robert Atchley's studies on retirement (Atchley, 1975) lead him to believe that women have more trouble at retirement than do men. In spite of the common assumption that women can always go back to their families, most women work precisely because they don't have a family to go back to, at least in terms of a fulfilling occupation.

Grandparenting is not all that important to most women. Neugarten and Weinstein (1964) studied five styles of grandparenting and found that in older years, the most frequent form is the distant grandparent, or the occasional one. Older people—older women—often say, "It's great to see the grandchildren come, but it's great to see them go." Relationships between grandparents and grandchildren tend to be contingent on the middle generation, unless they live close to each other and form a direct bond. Furthermore, the middle-generation linkage is usually a woman.

CASSANDRA COMPLEX

I think middle-aged women have a "Cassandra complex." They are worriers. They have been socialized to affiliations; women are more affiliative than men. Most women can name five best friends, and these are really best friends with whom they share secrets and on whom they rely for advice and help. Men, when they say they have a best friend, usually name their wife. Men, therefore, tend to be quite disabled if they are widowed. When their wife dies, they are apt to remarry quickly because their linkage, even with their own children, is through their wife.

Thus women, the worriers and affiliators, are worrying about all the members of their family. Middle-aged women watch their husbands carefully, because men get heart attacks at this age, and notoriously don't take care of themselves—partly because stereo-typical masculinity is equated with strength and vigor. But it is all right for their wives to make doctor's appointments for them or remind them to take their medicine so long as they are obliging her whims and not acknowledging their own fears. The Neugarten, et al. (1963) study of menopause found that it was true the women at this age were concerned about health, but it was their husband's health, not their own.

Middle-aged women not only worry about their husbands, they also worry about their children. Neugarten (1968) refers to the "social clock." Age restrictiveness is strongest—the social clock is most demanding—for youth. Young people are supposed to get jobs; they're supposed to get married. This means that if they don't their mothers feel they have failed. And today, with so many delayed marriages, childbearing, and even career onsets, many middle-aged mothers are worrying. Meanwhile, they're monitoring and helping their aging parents and parents-in-law. Should nursing homes be considered? Or a move into their own homes?

PERSONALITY

While teenagers become progressively more sex-typed, in middle age people start de-differentiating. Men reassume these so-called feminine characteristics they had dropped during adolescence, while women reassume their earlier characteristics labeled masculine. Because they are no longer inhibiting vital aspects of their personality, they become more spontaneous and vital. Men can allow themselves to be more introspective, more sensitive, more tender; women more assertive and strong. Livson (1976) analyzed the Berkeley longitudinal data on the sample that had been followed from childhood to middle age. She found that all the men had become more androgynous (combining both the "masculine" and "feminine" traits that fitted their own unique pattern), and that a panel of clinical psychologists who read their records judged them all to be in good mental health. Those women who had taken on the masculine characteristics they had dropped by nineteen were also judged to be in good mental health, but the other women, who stayed ultrafeminine, were evaluated as anxious and depressed. Their twelve year-old records incidentally showed these nonchangers to be girls who were most anxious and depressed at that time.

Pauline Bart (1970) studied women who became mentally ill in middle age. She labeled them "Mother Portnoys." They had become too specialized into a "feminine role," and were so involved with their home and children that the maturing of these children left them stranded.

A final cautionary note: women who are now old may not represent future generations of old people. There are powerful generational effects. If we describe women who are now old as relatively poor, dumb, ugly, and unimportant, we may not describe their daughters and grandaughters, when they get to be old, in the same terms. All our present planning for old age had better take into account the probability that we will be dealing with different kinds of people and conditions.

•   •   •

SUMMARY

I have touched on several issues in the social situation of present day older women. One deals with the relevance of existing norms, stereotypes, and biases relating to both sex and age. A second issue is the validity of the negative stereotype that older women are poor, dumb, and ugly—and unimportant. A third point involves the special quality of relations of older women—or middle-aged women—to their families. They are the affiliators and worriers—the Cassandras— and if they still have a husband in old age, usually put him as of first importance and children next. They are reciprocally of special importance to their husband and children, though maybe out of commitment and obligation-attachment than fun-attraction.

REFERENCES

Atchley, R. *The sociology of retirement.* Cambridge, Mass.: Schenkman, 1975.

Bart, P. Mother Portnoy's complaint. *Transaction.* November-December, 1970, 69-74.

Bernard, J. *The future of marriage.* New York: Bantam Books, 1973.

Candy, S. A comparative analysis of friendship functions in sex age groups of men and women. Unpublished Ph.D. dissertation, Wayne State University, 1977.

Cummings, E., & Henry, W. *Growing old: The process of disengagement.* New York: Basic Books, 1961.

Feldman, H. Development of the husband-wife relationship. Ithaca, N.Y.: Cornell University, 1964.

Hill, R., Foote, N., Aldous, J., Carlson, R., & Macdonald, R. *Family development in three generations.* Cambridge, Mass.: Schenkman, 1970.

Livson, F. Patterns of personality development in middle-aged women: A longitudinal study. *International Journal of Aging and Human Development,* 1976, *7* (2), 107-115.

Lowenthal, M., Thurnher, M., & Chiriboga, D. *Four stages of life.* San Francisco: Jossey-Bass, 1975.

McKain, W. Retirement marriage. Storrs, Conn.: University of Connecticut Agriculture Experiment Station, 1969.

Neugarten, B., Wood, V., Kraines, R., & Loomis, B. Women's attitudes toward the menopause. *Vita Humana,* 1963, *6,* 140-151.

Neugarten, B. *Middle age and aging.* Chicago: University of Chicago Press, 1968.

Neugarten, B., & Weinstein, K. The changing American grandparent. *Journal of Marriage and the Family,* 1964, *26,* 199-204.

Nowak, C. Youthfulness, attractiveness and the midlife woman: An analysis of the appearance signal in adult development. Presented at Midwestern Psychological Association, 1976.

Parron, E. Relationships of black and white golden wedding couples. Unpublished Ph.D. dissertation, Rutgers University, 1979.

Troll, L. The family of later life: A decade review. *Journal of Marriage and the Family,* 1971, *33,* 263-90.

Troll, L., & Bengtson, V. Generations in the family. In W. Burr, R. Hill, F.I. Nye, & I. Reiss (Eds.) *Contemporary theories about the family.* New York: Free Press, 1979, 127-161.

Troll, L., Miller, S., & Atchley, R. *Families of later life.* Belmont, Calif.: Wadsworth, 1978.

Chapter 3

SOCIAL CLASS AND THE OLDER FAMILY MEMBER

Natalie P. Trager

There are all levels of sophistication in attempts to define "social class." The social indicators most commonly explored, at least in research in America, are level of income and of education. Very few researchers, to my knowledge, have attempted to explore attributed status, except in a sexist approach; i.e., females define themselves in relation to the males in their lives—fathers, husbands, sons. Yet, attributed or inherited social class is a very real social indicator, particularly in special enclaves of Massachusetts, Virginia, Georgia, and California. To be a descendent of a "first family" still confers social status in some groups. I have met and marveled at many old Southern ladies, surrounded by memorabilia of past family exploits, who eke out a barely adequate existence on S.S.I.; but their self-image is that of a member of an elite. These ladies have shown me their hand-painted china cups, "done by my great-grandmother, who was second cousin to dear Tom Lee, you know." Social class? These ladies were poor and poorly educated, but considered themselves, and were considered by the community, to be in the upper stratum.

Assignment by the community to a particular social class appears to depend on someone else's value judgment of an individual. "An individual is only powerful or powerless in relation to another individual or individuals." (Bell and Newby, 1976). If these old ladies, by some combination of unlikely circumstances, were forced to move to an apartment/hotel in Chicago, their hand-painted cups would contribute nothing positive to their assignment to a social class. The ladies would be judged by the usual socioeconomic variables accepted in the Midwest. These variables include occupational history, educational level achieved, and income level. The last variable appears to be complicated by from what source the individual receives a given sum. Interest, dividends, pensions, annuities, and rentals appear to confer more attributed status than do savings withdrawals, sale of possessions, support from relatives, social security, and/or public assistance. Thus, our mythical southern ladies transplanted to Chicago would be abruptly precipitated from high to low-status persons: they have never worked outside the home, they are minimally educated, and their income is from public (federal) assistance. Tom Lee? Who ever heard of him? What's he got to do with anything?

Our ladies have lost a crucial item: some present power over their environment. The material resources at their disposal assign them to low class status in their new environment. It appears to me that this one variable—ability to influence one's environment—is what is really meaningful. Whether the aged live alone, with a spouse or relatives, or in an institution, the level of happiness or contentment appears to be a reflection of the presence or absence of behavioral self-determination.

There is no real doubt that those goals which attract young people (good health, energetic living, independence) are also important objectives for older people (Palmore, 1969). Most of us begin to lose our "good health" during the decade of the fifties; by the sixties we are coping with our various physical decrements (arthritis, increasing deafness, diminishing eyesight, erratic digestive and bowel function) by voluntarily restricting our "energetic living." The desire and need for independence, however, remains with most aged persons.

I remember how disgusted a young administrator of aging programs was when his office surveyed a goodly sample of aged persons in Michigan and asked, among other questions, "What would you do with an outright gift of $2,000?", and a majority of the aged answered, "Buy a prepaid funeral." This, to him, indicated how unrealistic and "senile" most old people are. He completely ignored the real message: i.e., maintaining independence, even to the final rites, is a culturally valued goal for the aged.

The amount of behavioral self-determination available to the aged varies by the factors of past employment, sex, and subculture. Different roles are effected differentially (Bengston, 1967). The old plumber doesn't disengage from his trade; too many persons clamor for his services. On the other hand, the retired systems analyst is outmoded; his services are unneeded. (Artists, both male and female, rarely retire; they are compulsive workers; growing old is usually accompanied by increased expertise.) Some elderly males have measured their self-worth all their lives by the existence of a weekly paycheck. It is not impossible that the sixty-five year-old retired banker of high socioeconomic status may envy his sixty-five year-old Spanish-American gardner of low socioeconomic status who can pick and choose among the many jobs offered him. This matter of choice, of power over one's environment, is the essence of morale or happiness in the majority of aged males. By the year 2000, when our present middle-aged males turn sixty-five, there will be even less need for their services, since jobs are increasingly mechanized, even in the professions.

As a logical consequence to the culturally-prized value system under which most aged females have lived their entire lives, the most important morale factor reported by numerous studies (Havighurst, 1976; Treas, 1977; Johnson & Bursk, 1977) is the possibility (by choice) of social involvement, with family members first, friends second, and the community (church, etc.) third. Females defined the extent of social interaction as their prime measure of self-regard. Females appear to suffer more than males when displaced late in life (Havighurst, 1976). There is support for the proposition that early adult life has more relevance for the aging life styles of men than of women. (Maas & Kuypers, 1974). This may be the natural concomitant to the fact that most females' prestige is limited to a very restricted reference group of family, friends, and neighbors. The older the female the more geographically restricted she may be in social contacts. Many aged females develop surrogate relationships with the heroes and heroines of soap operas.

The leading American researcher in the field of widowhood, Helena Lopata, has contributed considerable data on elderly females in relation to social class. One surprising item, considering the stereotypical expectation that social life collapses once a female is widowed, is that 43 percent of the widows in her study (1975) reported no change in social life. However, other items reinforce the idea that the elderly widow is socially restricted, regardless of class.

An upper-class widow, judged by educational level and life style, finds herself severely disorganized at the loss of her husband. Luckily, her superior resources make it easier to put her life together again. Widows of all classes report that the "fifth wheel syndrome" constrains their activity. They feel awkward dining in restaurants where most patrons are couples. The work-group colleagues of the dead husband no longer sustain any contact; often, even in-laws no longer keep in touch. Many widows, of all classes, find that the American belief that friendships last a lifetime find that an extra female, past marriageable or sex-seductive age, has lost friendships as well as her husband.

Reactions to aging vary not only as a function of social class, but reflect ethnic group membership as well. For example, elderly Spanish-American men and women prize privacy and independence. By choice, no one asks for advice or help from an agency (unless forced) because such action reflects adversely upon family solidarity and competence (Madsen, 1964). A high value is placed on immediate personal contact. They live closer to their children than most Anglos, and have more contact with little children and friends. While most Spanish-Americans are illiterate in both Spanish and English, have low level jobs and housing, and other elements of a low socioeconomic class, their measurement of morale is determined by their success in close, warm family relationships, independently maintained. Elderly females spend most of their leisure-time activity with other females.

Elderly Jews in the U.S.A., at least those served by Jewish agencies, appear to have many conflicts with their middle-aged children. There is usually a marked difference in socieconomic and educational status between the two generations (Simos, 1970) with the children generally higher on the ladder than the parents. Most disputes erupt over housing; the children want aged parents to acquiesce in any housing arrangement selected for them by the bill-paying generation. Planning to include aging parents in social or family affairs on a consistent and prolonged basis is rarely welcomed by the middle-aged children. The elderly Jew, expecting traditional lifelong respect and care from children, resents being told where to live and how to behave.

Aged black men and women in the United States appear to retain independence of living longer than aged whites (*Gerontologist,* 1972). Whether they live with a spouse, as a single person, or as a boarder with a relative, aged blacks appear to live as they please, restricted only by inadequacies of income or health-related mobility. Some of this aura of free choice may, ironically, be attributable to earlier, societal discrimination: many elderly black men and women have worked all their lives in uncovered employment and have no official earning record with Social Security. The Supplemental Security Income program, until recently, covered all persons seventy-two years or older even if they had no officially legitimized earnings record. Hence, many elderly blacks, for the first time in their lives, had a guaranteed minimum income plus Medicaid benefits, food stamps, and access to other programs for the aged such as the Title VII communal meal program.

Let's not forget, either, that a contribution of $100.00 per month to a young black family whose take-home income is only $400.00 a month will increase their capacity to survive. The aged family member living with relatives has made a substantial contribution, accounting for 20 percent of the total family income. This helps to buy dignity, freedom from obligation and can sweeten the care burden on the younger couple who may be attempting to pay college tuition for their children. (By contrast, the average white family wage is about $16,000 and rising; $1,200 a year from an aged parent increases a white family's spending capacity by only .075 percent.) Black elderly men and women are, in general, strong in body and mind (Darcy, 1977). They usually have a large store of common sense, serene religious faith, and an optimistic outlook. These characteristics are not statistically bound to any socioeconomic level.

There may be research concerning the relations between siblings in the latter years which holds social class constant, but I have been unable to locate any. In fact, I found very little which inquires into elderly sibling relationships. One study (Bultema, 1969) reports that low-class elderly siblings have little contact with each other. The middle-class elderly sibling does increase contact after death of spouse and/or retirement. Middle-class elderly sisters appear to develop fairly close contacts as they grow older.

The sparsity of such data leads to speculation about future research, especially considering demographic projections concerning the United States population mix. We already have four and five generation families, all alive at the same time, an entirely new phenomenon. If current predictions regarding longevity research breakthroughs come true we will have six and seven generations living at the same time. If we tie this fact in with the growing popularity of serial marriage, it may be that emotional support in old age could more and more become a function of siblings rather than of children and grandchildren.

Simply put, demographic change has reduced the number of descendants to whom an older person can look for assistance (Treas, 1977). Endemic inflation is rapidly decreasing the capacity of the aged to pay their own bills; there may well be two generations (great-great-grandparents, great-grandparents) living in custodial facilities, grandparents living on retirement income, parents (both working) struggling to pay bills for college tuitions, and young adults raising babies, unable to contribute to anyone's bills but their own. We certainly cannot rely on sentiment; there will be inevitable growth of governmental intervention in the care of the aged. Eventually, government may pay children to take care of their aged parents, just as government now pays welfare mothers to take care of their children.

There has been some class-tied research on attitudes toward elderly family members held by adolescents and young adults (Ivester & King, 1977; Salter & Salter, 1976; Templer, Ruff, & Franks, 1971). Middle-class, white, eighteen year-olds do not appear to be "turned off" by elderly people. In fact, there is some evidence that their own latent death anxiety (much higher in females than males) leads to more positive attitudes and behavior towards the elderly. This positive attitude does not appear to be related to actual contact with grandparents; a study done in 1975 (Ivester & King) where the average age of students tested was fifteen, shows attitudes toward the aged to be positive whether or not grandparents were available for interaction. While middle-class white students reported a more positive attitude than lower-class black students, it was a very small difference, statistically insignificant.

The utilization rate of long term care facilities can also be distinguished. I should like to review some of the major findings of class-tied research about the aged family member and use of such facilities.

In Baltimore, (Vandetti & Gelfand, 1976) first, second, and third-generation Americans (Italian, Catholic, or Polish ancestry) were interviewed. Fifty percent of the respondents stated they preferred to place a bedridden parent in a church-sponsored rather than a government-sponsored facility. The language barrier between aged ethnic persons and professional staff was cited as a major source of worry. The respondents most receptive to placing aged parents or grandparents in any home was positively correlated with the number of years of education and the level of income: i.e., the more educated and financially secure these lower middle-class persons become the more positively they view institutionalization of aged relations as a reasonable response to on-going care demands.

A Boston study (Johnson & Bursk, 1977) interviewed white middle-class adults, all twenty-one years of age or older (39 percent Yankees, 26 percent Jewish, 22 percent Irish, 13 percent Other; 39 percent Protestant, 35 percent Catholic, 20 percent Jewish, 6 percent Other). The respondents reported a good affective relationship with an aging parent where "the parents are engaged and busy in various activities." Respondents also scored high on desire for "respite care facilities" (promise of free weekends and vacations) to serve parents who live in homes of young adults. Again, as the level of education and financial security rises, young adults are more receptive to institutionalization.

However, these studies (and others in similar vein) appear to be simplistic in cause/effect analysis if we consider studies which focus on those factors that actually effect family involvement in nursing home care (Brody, et al., 1978). Most families provide strong support to aged parents "if strong, integrative relationships with other family members existed prior to the onset of illness." The never-married, divorced, childless and poor old person is usually prematurely admitted to nursing facilities. Barney (1977) found that 43 percent of admissions in her sample of Detroit homes were not really very sick, but had no other place to live where minimal supportive care was available. We find aged persons living in the community, alone, or with a spouse, or with a relative, who have much higher degrees of disability than the average nursing home resident. Housing such people is the critical variable; without a care unit (spouse and/or children), placement in an institution remains the placement preferred by those professionals charged with the responsibility of caring for the aged. Thus we have the phenomenon of relatively mobile and physically competent aged being assigned to beds designated for severely disabled persons.

It appears that cracks in the family structure are widening. The cult of individualism, the recognition of manifold rights of anyone physically and financially able to assert them, is slowly but surely overcoming sentimental obligations. Aged persons themselves declare their right to be independent, to make their own choices, not to be a burden on their children. All of our cultural norms, values and roles effect the expectations of older people, including relationships with adult children. How long will we be able to assume that 75 percent (Brody, et al., 1978) of all aged parents needing care will continue to receive it from a family unit?

Home care of a mentally handicapped old person is quite different from care of a physically handicapped old person. Here is the rub when families try to take care of aged relatives. Families feel guilty and angry, unable to accept the reality of irreversible brain damage (organic brain syndrome) and the resulting memory loss, eccentric or bizarre behavior, wandering, and general disorientation. The two most common causes of OBS are alcoholism and atherosclerosis, with Alzheimer's disease also contributing its share of premature and progressive senile dementia. It is estimated that in 1977 there were 810,000 senile aged living in mental hospitals, nursing homes, or in the community (Wershaw, 1977). While this is only .037 percent of the total aged population, the amount of public and private resources required to care for this aged subset of the population constitutes a heavy burden.

What effect does the social class of the aged family person have on nursing home aides, charge nurses and doctors, particularly in cases of senile dementia? Most studies, whether conducted by gerontologists (Thorson, 1974) or professional nursing personnel (Gillis, 1973) are remarkably consistent in results: i.e, there is no effect, pro or con, from race or income; the strongest factor is the number of years of education completed by staff persons. There was a very clear dividing line between those without post-secondary education and those with one or more years of college; the more education, the more positive attitude toward aging.

Practitioners in the field of care of the sick elderly become tangled in the fantastic array of heterogeneity encountered in meeting their needs. Cuban-Americans honor aged parents and are disgusted with families who "put their old people into homes to get rid of them." Anglos honor aged parents and "take care of them until they die." American Indians honor aged parents and "leave them alone." Young family members who all their lives have been brainwashed by the "magic pill" philosophy sold on television are apt to think of aging as something which can be reversed if Grandpa or Grandma will only find the right combination of doctor and treatment. Middle-aged family members, harassed by debt and inflation, are apt to settle for X dollars per month to "help out." Aged family members, experiencing the inevitable sensory decrements of age, living on inadequate but fixed incomes, react according to their own particular expectations developed over the life span.

How important to survival is freedom of choice? A 1977 study (Noelker & Harvel, 1978) reports that among those nursing home residents who reported that they preferred to live elsewhere than in the home where they were interviewed, the percentage of death 2 years later was twice as great compared to residents who had chosen to live in the facility.

To return to the first major statement of these remarks, that aged family members, above all, require autonomy of behavioral choice to achieve life satisfaction; how much influence does "social class," per se, have in assuring a high level of life satisfaction? Certainly socioeconomic history is not a simple guideline, since the aged may be "newly poor" (the retiree with a 50 percent cut in income) or "newly well-off" (the black retiree on SSI). Status in old age is a mixture of present and past. Paul Cameron (1972) expressed it this way:

> Two factors—membership in social class and personal life history—are probably not equally weighted in arriving at an appraisal of happiness. One's social class is probably 'ground,' and one's personal life history 'figure' in the judgment. (p. 121)

"Ground" (e.g., Jewish-American, Italian-American, WASP, Spanish-American) changes, but very slowly. Each cohort born at a particular moment of our history shares common "historical ground;" yet each cohort ages in a different way. WASPS born 1910-1920 share some common ground with WASPS born 1920-1930, but expectations of the proper roles for an aging family member had been altered by the impact of World War I, Prohibition, Women's Suffrage, the Crash of 1929, and other events of that decade. More recent cohorts of WASPS still share common "ground" with these other cohorts, but are heir to slow but far-reaching social changes in educational process, in nutrition, in occupation, and political nurturing. Each new cohort born has its own "field," characterized by sex, genetic traits, and family background. Since each of us is preoccupied with our own "field," we tend to expect other members of our age cohort to believe and hold expectations similar to our own.

Matilda Riley contributed a chapter to the Fall 1978 issue of *Daedalus* titled "Aging, Social Change and the Power of Ideas." It is a beautifully reasoned and succinct statement of the interplay of "ground" and "field" and the impact the present young and middle-aged cohorts can have when they become the aged of the future. As individuals, each of us can modify our own process of aging, can upgrade our expectations. To quote Dr. Riley:

> There is scope for us, personally and as members of the changing society, to benefit from the understanding that the process of aging is neither inexorable nor immutable, that to a considerable degree we ourselves are in control. (p. 50)

The earlier we start the process of control over our own aging the better. There is little argument about the notion that people do not suddenly change in their middle and later years. We are the result of what we have been, as children, as adolescents, as young adults. We end up as our behavioral choices, over the years, have propelled us. It is generally accepted, in the literature, that successfully aging men and women follow a life-style pattern of long duration, with pathology, when it occurs, being telegraphed much earlier in the life cycle of the individual. Erikson claims that how a person deals with old age regardless of social class is similar to the manner in which he dealt with earlier crises of his life. Piaget's developmental theory of the growth of learning mechanisms has speculated that the high school student's idiosyncratic behavior is mirrored in the kindergartener. We might also say that the old man or woman is mirrored in the young adult, male or female.

REFERENCES

Barney, J. The Prerogative of Choice in Long-Term Care. *Gerontologist, 1977,* 17, 309-314.

Bell, C., & Newby, H. Husbands and Wives: the Dynamics of the Deferential Dialectic. In D. Barker & S. Allen (Eds.), *Dependence and Exploitation in Work and Marriage,* New York: Longman, Inc., 1976, Chapter 8, p. 152.

Bengston, V.L. Occupational and rational differences in patterns of role activity and life satisfaction: a cross-national pilot study. Paper presented at the 20th annual meeting of the Geronological Society, St. Petersburg, Florida, November, 1967.

Brody, S.J., Poulshock, W., & Masciocchi, C.F. The Family Caring Unit: A Major Consideration in the Long-Term Support System. *Gerontologist,* Vol. 18, No. 6, December 1978, 556-561.

Bultema, G.L., Life Continuity and Morale in Old Age. *Gerontologist,* Part I, Winter 1969, 251-253.

Cameron, P. The Generation Gap: Time Orientation. *Gerontologist,* Vol. 12, No. 2, Part I, Summer 1972, 121.

Dancy, Jr. *The Black Elderly: A Guide for Practitioners.* Ann Arbor, Michigan: University of Michigan/Wayne State University Institute of Gerontology, 1977.

Gillis, Sr. M. Attitudes of Nursing Personnel Toward the Aged. *Nursing Research,* 1973, *22,* 517-520.

Havighurst, R.J., & Neugarten, B. Family and Social Support. *Gerontologist,* Vol. 16, No. 1, Part II, February 1976, 63-69.

Hollingshead, A. *Two-Factor Index of Social Position. New Haven, Connecticut: 1957, (copyright held by authors).*

Invester, C., & King, K. Attitudes of Adolescents Toward the Aged. *Gerontologist,* Vol. 17, No. 1, February 1977, 85-89.

Johnson, E.S., & Bursk, B. Relationships Between the Elderly and their Adult Children. *Gerontologist,* Vol. 17, No. 1, February 1977, 90-96.

Lambing, M.L. Leisure-Time Pursuits Among Retired Blacks by Social Status. *Gerontologist,* Vol. 12, Winter 1972, November 4, 363-367.

Lopata, H. Couple-Companionate Relationships in Marriage and Widowhood. In N. Glazer-Malbin (Ed). *Old Family/New Family.* New York: D. Van Nostrand Co., Chapter 5, 1975.

Maas, H.S., & Kuypers, J.A. *From Thirty to Seventy.* San Francisco: Jossey-Bass, 1974, 108.

Madsen, W. *The Mexican-Americans of South Texas.* New York: Holt, Rinehart & Winston, 1964.

Noelker, L. & Harvel, Z. Predictors of Well-Being and Survival Among Institutionalized Aged. *Gerontologist,* Vol. 18, No. 16 (1978) 562-567.

Palmore, E. Predicting Longevity: A Follow-up Controlling for Age. *Gerontologist,* Part I Winter 1969, 248.

Riley, M.W. Aging, Social Change, and the Power of Ideas. *Daedalus,* Fall 1978, 39-52.

Salter, C.A., & Salter, C. Behaviors toward the Elderly among Young People as a Function of Death Anxiety. *Gerontologist,* Vol. 16, No. 3, June 1976, 232-236.

Simos, B. Relation of Adults with Aging Parents. *Gerontologist,* Vol. 10, No. 2, Summer 1970, 135-139.

Templer, D.I., Ruff, C.F., & Franks, C.M. Death Anxiety: Age, Sex, and Parental Resemblance in Diverse Populations. *Developmental Psychology, 1971, 4,* 108.

Thorson, J.A. Attitudes toward the Aged as a Function of Race and Social Class. *Gerontologist,* August 1975, 343-344.

Treas, J. Family Support Systems for the Aged: Some Social and Demographic Considerations. *Gerontologist,* Vol. 17, No. 6, December 1977, 486-491.

Vandetti, D.V. & Gelfand, D.E. Attitudes of White Ethnic Families. *Gerontologist,* Vol. 16, No. 6, December 1976, 544-549.

Wershaw, H.J. Some Thoughts about Senility. *Gerontologist,* Vol. 17, No. 4, August 1977, 297-302.

Chapter 4

THE ABUSED OLDER WOMAN
A Discussion of Abuses and Rape

Eloise Rathbone-McCuan

An explicit assumption reflected in previous chapters is that to be old and female is to live with multiple forms of vulnerability, and in this chapter the particular types to be considered include older women who have been, or who are potential victims of one of either of two forms of intra-family violence and/or rape. It describes and analyzes the various conditions faced by older women when they are endangered through the intentional actions of other persons that place them at risk and in some situations even threaten their continued survival. Intervention and service provision issues will be reviewed in relation to spouse abuse, potential abuse, and the rape of older women.

There are four trends, now converging, that have stimulated the emerging of concern about the victimization of older women as there is recognition and concern about: 1) the general criminal victimization of older persons; 2) the gross limitations of current protective service laws and programs; 3) the impact of intra-family violence on female family members; and 4) the consequences of all forms of

cultural violence for American women. These areas have been researched to various degrees, but limited attention has been given to
an integration of findings relevant to the older woman. Controversy
exists among professionals regarding whether or not the general
victimization of older people in the United States constitutes a crisis
situation (Davis & Brody, 1979). In testimony before the House
Select Committee on Aging (April 28, 1976), three theories regarding
vitimization were set forth:

1. Older people are victimized in the same proportion as the
   general population.
2. Older people are victimized proportionately more than the
   general population.
3. Older people are "over victimized by some crimes, "under-
   victimized" by others, and are victimized proportionately the
   same for others.

To the extent that the older woman possesses the characteristics
of physical or mental impairment, poverty, aloneness, dependence on
walking and public transportation, poor housing conditions, and
routine predictable behaviors, she is vulnerable to victimization
(Davis & Brody, 1979). The special vulnerabilities of the older
women to rape or other physical assaults may be summarized as
follows:

1. Her normal physical capacities may be diminished, thus restricting her ability to escape, defend herself, or identify her as-
   sailant. She may also suffer from a variety of physical or mental
   impairments which render her unable to use complicated pre-
   cautions against victimization and make her virtually helpless if
   assaulted.
2. Many older women have set routines which are easily ob-
   servable to potential assailants. Habits of banking, shopping,
   and hours of coming and going are predictable, thereby facilitating the planning of a burglary, robbery, or rape.
3. The vulnerability of an older woman is increased further if she
   is dependent on walking or public transportation. It also increases chances for fraud, confidence games, and being observed and followed for purposes of robbery or rape.

4. Most older women in the urban settings do not live alone. In addition, most have some network of social support. There are many, however, who are alone or who live in poverty in run-down, high-crime areas. These particular older women are the most vulnerable to victimization and are, in fact, frequently and repeatedly preyed upon by assailants or burglars who may also be their neighbors. Their jeopardy is compounded if they are physically or mentally impaired (Davis & Brody, 1979).

Before proceeding to a discussion of the three particular forms of victimization, it may be useful for the reader to examine the similar and different characteristics among abuse of the older spouse; abuse of the aged mothers by their adult children or other family members, and the rape of older women. (Table 1) The characteristics presented are based on a combination of published clinical and empirical research, case material gathered by the author and consultation with practitioners working with younger and older women who are victims of abuse and/or rape. It is considered to be a preliminary effort by the author to show some basic similarities that warrant further investigation, to provide a framework for analyzing similarities and differences in these three forms, and to make specific and general recommendations regarding intervention.

Spouse Abuse Among Older Women

With growing public awareness of the problem of spouse abuse, the victimized spouse is more apt to seek help, and as a result, more data are becoming available and more research is being done on this topic (Johnson, Ferry, & Kravitz, 1978). Research studies support the contention that wife beating is a phenomenon common to all age, racial, class, and economic groups (Fields, 1976). However, this body of information tends to overlook the variable of the chronological age of the victim in relation to her developmental stage and other age-related variables that may be relevant to her seeking assistance, benefiting from intervention, and avoiding a reoccurance of the abuse. Much of what has been written about spouse abuse needs to be re-examined in relation to the age and developmental stage of the victim, particularly if we are to understand the problems and needs of older wives who are victims.

Table 1

Characteristics of Spouse Abuse, Parental Abuse and Rape Abuse Among Older Women

CHARACTERISTICS	TYPE OF ABUSE		
	SPOUSE ABUSE	PARENTAL ABUSE	RAPE ABUSE
Female victim may be of various age and SES levels or different racial, ethnic, or religious groups	X	X	X
The abuse activity occurs most frequently in the residential setting	X	X	X
Patterns of general cultural violence may be directly/indirectly associated	X	X	X
Throughout middle age and late life the woman remains a potential victim	X	X	X
It may be a single or repeated event	X	X	X
There is a major likelihood of lasting physical and/or psychological consequences	X	X	X
The reported prevalence of all forms of abuse is under-estimated	X	X	X
The woman may be unwilling to leave the residential setting/living arrangement	X	X	X
Victims are reluctant to approach helping sources	X	X	X
There is a likelihood of another criminal activity taking place at the same time			X
The abuser is likely to be male	X		X
Likely the victim will know the abuser well	X	X	
It is a form of intra-family violence	X	X	

The term "battered women" refers to adult women who have been intentionally physically abused in ways which cause pain and/or injury; women who were forced into involuntary action or restrained by force from voluntary action by adult men with whom they have or had established relationships, whether or not within a legally married state (Pagelow, 1977). It is assault without theft in which the offender was the victim's spouse or ex-spouse and it occurs most frequently in the home at night and over the weekend (Gaguin, 1978). The rates of abusive events range widely from daily to twice a year (Flynn, 1977). For some women it occurs as a single incident and for others it is repeated and systematic. While marital rape is not often considered a legal crime, it is surely one of several forms of spouse abuse (Gelles, 1977) that goes unreported and the victim not assisted.

There is little data available regarding the differential patterns of the continuation of violent marriage among women. It is the author's hypothesis that the variation in patterns of marital situational continuation may be in part associated with the age of the spouse. If an older woman has lived with an abusing spouse for many years the pattern may become normative. She accepts her battering as a proper expression and response of her spouse to stress and thus may be less likely to defend or remove herself from the situation. Also, the longer that the marital couple have engaged in this pattern of behavior, the more routinized the battering the more it becomes part of the couples's behavioral repertoire.

Based on interviews with older women experiencing nonviolent related marital problems, the author is struck by the repeated acceptance of traditional subservient role patterns among older and elderly wives that legitimate dominating spouse behaviors. Simply stated, these women accept with little question that their husbands will continue to dominate them in ways that have existed throughout the marriage. They accept that the personal behaviors and characteristics of their husbands are not likely to change and/or do not necessitate change. These women often verbalize such attitudes as: "He's always been that way;" "I married him that way and he won't change now;" "It must be my fate to have been stuck with a man like him;" and "I guess he's as good a husband as any other." These statements represent a traditional ideology that may serve to maintain long-term violent marriages and discourage older women from seeking ways to change the marriage or to leave the relationship.

There has been little research on marital conflict resolution among older couples in the later stages of the family cycle or in changes in marital communication over long spans of marital life. The variable of the family's life cycle stage has been explored in relation to the continuation of the cycle when children, often victims of abuse and neglect in childhood marry and pass on their experience to their children (Steinmetz, 1977). Research on marital conflict has emphasized samples of two generations of nuclear families. Strauss surveyed 2,143 marital couples and studied their conflict resolution patterns. The sample was evaluated as being representative of all American couples (Steinmetz, 1979), but it provides no clear discussion of how the ages of the couple, the length of marriage, or the stage of the marital cycle may affect patterns of conflict resolution. There is as of yet no adequate data base to determine whether the general main factors which lead to acts of violence against a spouse vary with the chronological age and marital stage of the couple. The literature suggests several factors that lead to/are associated with marital violence:

1. The family as a social group is characterized by a high level of violence.
2. The United States, as a general practice, has used violence to maintain the status quo or achieve change.
3. Child rearing practices tend to be violent.
4. Violence within the family is legitimized.
5. The link between love and violence is established and violence is built into the most fundamental levels of personality.
6. Male dominance and the use of physical force to show it are accepted.
7. The sexual inequalities inherent in all of our societal systems leave women locked in a brutal marriage.

One point to be considered is the probability that women as they age or enter the old age period will be less likely to be victims of spouse abuse because of their changed marital status (e.g. widowhood, separation, or divorce). Statistics show that most marriages end before a woman reaches old age. Among women aged 65 and over in 1978, 52 percent were widowed; 3.2 percent were divorced and 6.2 percent were never married. Only 36.7 percent were married and living with their husbands in contrast to the 75 percent of older men who were married and living with their wives (King and Marvel, 1982). Therefore, the discussion of spouse abuse among older women is perhaps more directly relevant to middle-aged women in the midst of domestic situations where they are or could be a victim of spouse abuse. These women may be considered to be in important aging transitions. The victimization of middle-aged women may have relation to experiences in later life because there is continuity of life as a woman gradually ages. Events occurring earlier in the life course leave their marks, so that each individual enters old age with a particular set of skills, resources, relationships, and attitudes (Uhlenberg, 1979).

Despite the trauma experienced by some older women who are widowed or divorced in middle or later years, the author suspects that the death of the spouse or the shift in the relationship with the spouse through divorce may represent a release from continued violence from spouses, some emotional release from the burden and shame of a history of violence within their family, and/or a long-standing resentment of the spouse's abuse of children. This "relief of release" has become apparent to the author through data collected from oral histories and life review sessions with older women and conversations with adult children about the marital situations of their adult children. One middle-aged daughter who sought counseling regarding a nursing home placement for her aged mother stated:

> About the time I divorced my previous husband my father died. During the year that followed mother and I grew real close because we were both living through our pain together. We shared a lot of secrets. . . up until then I never knew that dad abused her when we were kids. That explains why at times I thought she hated him. . .I told her that she should have left him, but she said women of her generation didn't do that. . .We never talked about it again.

More data is becoming available about women's patterns of remaining in battering marriages. Walker (1979) proposed a three-stage process. First, there is a period of building tension for the abusing spouse during which the woman attempts placation. After the battering episode the husband is shamed and exhibits positive behaviors to the wife and she becomes prepared to wait for change. The development of a multivariate theory of battering will be an important contribution to the fields of psychology and criminal justice as more supporting evidence is established (Resick, 1983).

Perhaps the pattern of leaving the abusing spouse is an option seriously considered less often and undertaken less frequently by older as compared to younger wives. To label the behavior of a woman who returns to her home and her abusing spouse as sadomasochistic, is to deny the complexities of the social psychological and economic factors that may influence this decision and the varied impact these have on women. It is probable that conditions of emotional and financial dependency, fear of loneliness, and ignorance or rejection of alternative relationships affect decisions to stay or leave (Scott, 1974).

From a counseling perspective, the older a woman is the more ambivalent she may be about leaving a long-standing abusive marriage. An older woman may perceive that a long-standing marital relationship gives her security she won't find again because she won't have an opportunity to remarry; she fears loneliness to be a reality as her children have departed from their home to live independent lives; and the life of a single middle-aged woman is too threatening and socially devalued to consider. One worker recalled an aged husband who experienced arteriosclerotic rage reactions at the protestors in the Vietnamese War and beat his older wife, (by a second marriage), as a sort of catharsis. The woman gave no indication that she had considered leaving under these conditions.

The published references about the behavior of older abused wives are limited in number and narrow in scope. A study of 35 violent cases obtained from workers in a county welfare department made mention of a few cases of older women, classified as reluctant late disengagement types, struggling to decide about marriage payoffs and alternatives. In situations where the older woman decided to leave, the welfare agency provided emotional and financial support so that the ambivalent wife could stick by her decision (Pfouts, 1978). The article informs workers to be prompt, positive, and generous to these types of clients and points out the importance of immediate client access to supportive resources. The fewer resources a wife has and the less power she has, the more likely she is to stay with her violent husband (Gelles, 1976).

Empirical knowledge regarding clinical intervention with abused wives and/or marital counseling with the spouse and victim does not exist (Resick, 1983). An important point to emphasize is the need for a critical review of clinical methods being offered and an impartial analysis of their therapeutic values for women victims. The quality of research related to intervention with abused wives deserves serious examination regarding the validity and reliability of clinical intervention technologies, supportive community programs, and legalistic changes.

Abused wives are usually counseled alone. Abusing husbands often refuse to come for counseling when it is made available. Unfortunately, many shelters or crisis intervention programs for women do not offer outreach to spouses. This practice oversight should be recognized and changed. The range of intervention techniques for wives varies from self-help and consciousness-raising groups to traditional psychotherapy, but much emphasis is placed on crises intervention and emergency supportive services. Women wishing to leave the household with their children can be sheltered in a variety of settings for varying degrees of time. There they are protected, counseled, supported, and provided with legal, social, financial, and transitional supports. Some facilities offer specialized treatment to children and extend help to the abusing spouses. Sometimes shelters serve to relieve an overburdened court and police system. Some police departments have special police crises intervention units that work on the streets for primary intervention and prevention. Community task forces have been developed with goals to increase general public awareness, to develop better community resources, to plan and advocate for better legislation, and to change police and legal attitudes.

Battered Mothers

Popular magazines contain numerous references to the "battered parent syndrome." This is evidence of growing recognition that geriatric parental abuse is another form of intrafamily violence in our society. (Rathbone-McCuan and Hashimi, 1982; Rathbone-McCuan and Voyles, 1982). This type of abuse occurs outside of institutional settings even though the institutionalized elderly are potential victims of many types of abuse. In the human services, the term geriatric abuse has been applied to conditions of exploitation, emotional neglect, physical neglect, and actual abuse. Some circumstances/conditions of exploitation represent criminal acts against the elderly person committed by their adult children, but these actions often go unnoticed by the legal system. The issue of what is emotional neglect by adult children toward their aged parents is subject to individual and societal interpretation and there is little or no concensus. The vagueness and multiple meanings of geriatric parental abuses indicates need to develop definitional clarity.

Elderly men and women both are potential victims of abuse from adult children, but the phenomena is more prevalent among elderly women than men. This is because a greater proportion of women live into advanced old age only to suffer increased physical or mental impairment and thus depend upon their adult children. Perhaps the longevity of old women is sometimes viewed as more of a problem than a blessing. Married adult children, especially daughters, are sometimes seriously stressed and strained because of the dual responsibilities of family and older parental care-giving.

In this chapter the term "battered mother" refers to aged women who have been intentionally abused or physically neglected in ways which cause actual injury and/or place her in a life-endangering situation. These aged women are usually involuntarily and/or unknowingly forced or placed into the endangering circumstances by their adult children. This definition emphasizes the filial relationship between the victim and the abuser. The woman is a potential victim of family-related abuse from the cradle to the grave (Rathbone-McCuan, 1980). A list of characteristics found to be present in a series of case studies included:

1. The victim is female.
2. The victim is sixty-five years or older.
3. The victim is functionally dependent because of inadequate resources or functional limitations.
4. There is a history of alcoholism, retardation, or psychiatric illness for either the care-giver or elderly person.
5. There is a history of inter-and intra-generational conflict.
6. There is a previous history of related incidences.

The abuse is likely to take place in the home because many of these elderly women are housebound. Whether it occurs most frequently at night or during the weekends is not known. During the abuse episode there are probably few direct observers, and if there are, they often remain silent. The author believes that there may be a significant proportion of cases, especially among older women who live alone, where abusive action is not directly witnessed by others because there is no other person in the household. Depending upon how isolated the residence is from neighborhoods, especially in rural areas, neighbors may or may not have knowledge of the abuse. The explanations of why knowledgeable people remain silent, including the elderly person, involves fear, shame, and denial. It is the inability or the unwillingness of the aged victim to admit the abuse that makes identification and intervention difficult. There are instances when the absence of accusation on the part of the aged victim cannot be viewed simply as denial, particularly when woman's level of mental confusion is high or her fear of further consequences is greater than her hope that she will be helped.

Because of a lack of research, the inadequacy of case identification skills, and the isolation of older women victims, it is difficult to determine whether the greater proportion of cases are single or repeated episodes. Even if it is a single episode, the consequences can lead to the death of the aged victim. The author and other professionals would be comforted if they could believe that only a small proportion of cases involve multiple episodes, but there is no available data to support such a belief. If the general community is too quick to accept the "single incident"hypothesis this may further delay the public awareness and prevent service agencies from undertaking aggressive and comphrehensive outreach to these individuals.

It is important to note that this form of victimization is not an exclusive expression of male violence. The fact that women are more likely than men to be child abusers and that some women may behave violently toward husbands (Steinmetz, 1977) gives limited support to the possibility that adult female children may be responsible for the abusive actions toward elderly persons. That is particularly true if the stress of the care-giving functions contribute to some acts of violence, as daughters are more likely than sons to assume long-term and extensive care-giving functions to aged mothers.

It is of questionable value to speculate about the demographic characteristics of the abusing child until adequate research has been conducted to identify preliminary adult child abuser profiles. This author suggests that a priority of future research should be to determine how abusing adult children handle anger in situations that involve their aged mothers and what behaviors of the victim and environment factors provoke violence. This violent action represents maladaptive harmful behavior that can be prevented and/or changed. The most productive areas of research would focus on early case identification techniques, problem assessment approaches, and alternative intervention methods to protect the aged woman and help her adult child.

The following list indicates areas of assessment and possible targets for intervention for the battered mother that might be applied and then evaluated:

1. Determine if it is a single or repeated pattern of abuse on the part of the abuser. If it is a single event determine what can be done to prevent future events. Also examine for other forms of neglect.
2. Prepare a detailed description of abusive behavior (i.e. the kind of behavior and the extent of the damage).
3. Identifying the precipitating factors (i.e. verbal, nonverbal behaviors, situation where it occurs, behaviors previous to abusive interaction).
4. Determine the consequences of abusive behavior (i.e. what is the response of the abused person, what is the degree of the abuser in relation to the response of the abused).
5. Determine the abuser's level of emotional anger and problems of self-control related to the anger. The focus of intervention must be to change the environment and/or help the person control anger.
6. Determine if the abusive behavior is associated with other problems that may need to be the focus of some interventive effort in addition to other areas.

The major goal of such an interview would be to reconstruct the abusive episode, as it is likely that the person responsible for the case assessment and intervention plan will not have been there to observe the situation and, therefore, need to depend upon gathering the above important information through interview. The interview could be conducted in a variety of situations including the home, hospital, or office. If there were observers to the episodes these individuals should be interviewed. Whenever possible it is advantageous for the abused and the abuser to be interviewed at the same time. If problematic verbal interaction is involved samples of communication could be obtained (Thomas, 1977).

Clinical intervention can/should be focused on three general categories: 1)Interaction, 2) Self-management, and 3) Environmental change. In the area of interaction the clinician might focus on decision-making, problem-solving, and problems of verbal behavior. In self-management the clinician might help the abuser and/or the abused person work on emotional responses, assertiveness, and almost any other area that might help the individual gain better control over their responses. Efforts at environmental change could focus on a variety of areas ranging from self-care to obtaining a temporary legal guardianship or a protective service arrangement.

The brief guideline for intervention into the abusive behavioral problem indicates a concern for both the abused woman and the person responsible for the abuse. Single abuse episodes that come to the attention of social service personnel should not be ignored. This behavior, once it occurs, could be repeated and is an indication of highly stressful situations that the caregiver cannot cope with. A number of dysfunctional emotional states and behavior may characterize the abuser. For example: Fear and anxiety; anxiety/hostility, and contempt/shame; guilt; withdrawal; denial; scapegoating; and dependency (Voyles, 1979). The abuser deserves to be helped even though the priority of any crisis situation is to get the woman away from the situation for her own safety and protection.

There are behaviors among abused elderly women that serve as barriers for social service intervention. Some women want to believe that the adult child's abusive behavior will not continue and that there will be a change, and are therefore unwilling to leave despite their fear and ambivalence. At times, when the aged victim is presented with possible assistance from helping agencies, these are not accepted. One questionable assumption often made by practitioners is that this type of woman is mentally incompetent, but there is no empirical basis for this generalization among this specific group of aged victims. In cases where there is extensive mental dysfunction, workers may immediately opt to get the older woman out of her home through a declaration of legal incompetence. This approach often creates more problems for the aged woman. Too frequently, a certification of mental incompetency leaves the older person with no alternative but to be committed to a mental institution (Rathbone-McCuan, 1980).

The cases of life-endangering neglect that have come to the attention of service agencies often involve victims of advanced age, having outlived all close-kin family. These women, while not victims of the actions of filial abuse, per se, may end up in living arrangements with a more distant family member under conditions that produce a serious family situation. If older women are forced to live with more distant, often unfamiliar relatives, they may sense their lack of importance in relation to the other nuclear family members and their needs. It may be that the lack of importance within this "out of necessity" living arrangement contributes to low self-esteem and a willingness to accept the unacceptable.

Interventions can be provided by a range of different individuals including both professionals and other concerned persons. If there is resistance to intervention on the part of aged women, it can sometimes be reduced by providing help in a crisis situation. At the point of crisis, such basic care as food, clothing, medical care, in-home services, and transportation must be offered prior to the introduction of other clinical intervention for the abused or abuser.

Too few communities have resources immediately available to the victimized woman. This lack is associated with a larger problem of limited resources for aged persons who need a variety of protective services. Numerous states have been involved in the development of innovative comprehensive protective service programs for the elderly and in the passage of legislation that assures better service provision to the abused victim (Rathborn-McCuan and Hashimi, 1982). However, not all elderly women victims are fortunate to reside in communities where there are good crisis intervention services attached to a larger network of health, social, and economic supports that may be needed to generate permanent residential alternatives in a safer community environment. Legislation is usually an essential step for the development of such a service network (Rathbone-McCuan, E. and Hashimi, 1982).

Well organized advocacy networks for the abused and neglected elderly can do a great deal to raise the level of community awareness and undertake the lengthy process of advocating for better legislation (Hooyman, Rathbone-McCuan and Klingbeil, 1982). For example, the Missouri Association for Prevention of Adult Abuse is a statewide organization made up of professionals, elderly persons, and other citizens concerned about the inadequate legislation for older adults and the related service limitations of too few adult protective service workers, case referral mechanisms, short term residential opportunities, and interdisciplinary teams to make preliminary and on-going evaluation.

This social advocacy group has been the major force behind efforts to increase public concern about abused older persons and develop model service approaches if funds become available. The community surveys they have conducted, with the benefit of only minimal funds, have helped to clarify the serious and multiple problems confronting aged men and women. While these surveys have been directed toward determining the prevalence of many forms of abuse of elderly victims, they have obtained data to suggest that aged women who are physically abused, by children or other care givers, are also likely to be neglected. The distinction between physical abuse and physical neglect is often very vague, as consciously motivated or unmotivated neglect can result in immediate life endangering situations (Brot, 1978).

In Missouri the improvement of service resources is dependent upon the passage of legislation that will make economic resources available to provide the range of services both in specific communities and throughout the state. If the current Adult Protective Services legislative bill is passed by the Missouri legislature, the elderly women who are victims of intrafamily violence will be covered by this legislation under risk categories encompassing the aged persons who have suffered violence or danger from others and who remains at risk of further physical harm after the abusive episode has taken place. Comprehensive adult abuse legislation could be developed or amended to encompasss older and elderly women who are victims of spouse

abuse, battering from children, or rape. However, the passage of a
bill that attempts to meet the needs of all abused women may be less
popular in conservative states and have less success of passage.
Therefore, if multiple legislation is required to protect different
groups of adult women then new political coalition must be formed
between the advocate groups for women and the elderly. These are
natural and potentially very powerful alliances that can be of benefit
to older and elderly victims.

Rape As a Form Of Abuse Among Older Women

While there is little empirical information about the prevalence
and incidence of rape among older women, it is clear that older and
elderly women are victims and that specialized intervention and prevention programs are needed for older women. When communities
become interested in planning programs to provide services to female
victims of all ages, it is important to have at least a general statistical
profile of the prevalence and incidence rate in the community where
the program is proposed. In St. Louis, for example, there were 965
rapes in 1978, as compared to 920 rapes in 1977. On a per capita
basis the number of forcible rapes in the St. Louis area was 40.8 per
100,000 residents. For the entire state of Missouri, of the overall rate
of violent crimes, 1,360 were forcible rape. With increased local
police efforts to obtain better statistics on rapes, it may eventually be
possible to have more precise data with respect to the victims by age.

A recent study release by the National Institute of Mental
Health provides preliminary research about urban aged women as
victims or potential victims of rape. The authors have developed a
very complete guideline for prevention that covers planning and
implementing prevention programs, relevant rape avoidance
behaviors for older women, physical space design and security hard-
ware, alternative community organization approaches, educational/
training goals and materials (Davis and Brody, 1979). This report is a
major step in developing a basis for an expanded image of younger
female victims to include elderly women, and discusses why additional approaches are needed to make prevention effective for victims
of advanced age.

These authors (Davis and Brody, 1979) summarize the interrelationships of victimization, rape, and fear among older urban women as follows:

> Rape, although reported relatively less by older women, should be viewed as a crime that is generally underreported, especially by older women, and one that has a profound and probably permanent impact on the physical and psychological well-being of this especially vulnerable population. While it may not occur in epidemic proportions, it is a crime of extreme violation and, like homicide, must be controlled through protection planning regardless of prevalence.
>
> Fear of victimization is common among older women and, for the majority, provides an impetus to reduce activity or change to safer modes of accomplishing routine activities. Fear is especially common among poor urban women who live alone. They are, in fact, more often victimized than their peers who have more social and economic resources. The fear of the latter group may be well out of proportion to their chances of being victimized. Fear can be negative or positive, depending upon the reactions of individuals to the perceived threat. Planners of protection programs can reduce excessive negative fear through education and training programs. In addition, they can use realistic fear to build a health concern about the problem of victimization and an acceptance of the need for avoidance and protection activities.

The phenomenon of rape is a crime of violence, not passion, in which sex is used as a weapon. Rape has been the concern of many researchers, feminists, victims, and law enforcement officials, but not gerontologists. It is obvious that some specialized knowledge of and concern about the older woman who is a potential victim of rape should be included in any legal, education, and/or counseling program that is developed for meeting the multiple problems associated with rape among women of all ages, racial, economic, and geographic groups. The needs of the older woman may easily be overlooked or lost sight of given the lower rates of victimization among the population. Based on limited information with older women victims, their shame, guilt, and fear often make it difficult to get them to engage in legal actions involving future confrontation with a therapist, to verbalize their emotional conflicts even to very close intimates such as adult daughters and to take any steps including the use of counseling supports if these services could make their victimization more public.

Every community law enforcement unit, serving urban and rural communities needs some level of capability to deal with rape crimes. If small under-funded and under-staffed units in rural areas lack resources or staff expertise, they need to have appropriate consultation available at state expense. Urban units should be provided with sufficient resources to staff sex-crime sections of police departments in order to have at least minimally adequate coverage. Some states have taken progressive steps to improve the capacity of the criminal justice system to handle the problem of rape, but others have done little or nothing. The older victim is as affected by these systemic limitations as are other younger women. The more comprehensive a program including effective prosecution, community education, investigative capacities, cross-intervention, and counseling, the more likely that the needs of older women can be addressed.

The range of issues that affect younger female victims appear to have a compounded impact on older women because of their age, attitudes, and value systems. As a result the sexual nature of the crime is much harder to deal with and it is more difficult for the older victim to adjust. There may need to be some modifications in the counseling services offered to them. Briefly, these include:

1. A more direct, prompt, and personalized outreach to these older victims, conducted in the most private manner possible.
2. A greater application of rape counseling using an older victim to counsel an older victim. The supportive intervention available may require that the peer relation extend over a significantly longer period of time and be extended into helping the victim to reach a point where essential activities such as shopping, leisure activities in or out of the home, seeing a physician, can be reinstituted without overwhelming fear.
3. A more detailed preparation for jury trial proceedings that offer the older woman a more realistic picture of legal procedures and trial outcomes in order that she has an understanding of the

demands placed on her during the various legal stages, but has an intimate supportive relationship with legal counsel to help sustain her participation.

CONCLUSION

An implicit assumption that guided this comparative discussion of spouse abuse, maternal battering, and rape among older female victims is that: agism and sexism interact to place unique stresses on the physical and emotional well-being of older women who are victims of violence. These older women are likely to remain victims unattended by the health, mental health, and social service delivery systems. Too little is known about the help seeking behaviors of these older women because there appears to be a disproportionately low incidence of case reporting and/or case identification. Subjective impressions lead to preliminary hypotheses that older women are likely to make helping contacts with physicians because of the possibility that they have experienced a physical injury or been sufficiently traumatized to have reactive physical and emotional problems. Physicians are not well equipped to identify the relationship between the physical and emotional signs and symptoms and the causal event related to her violent victimization.

When the doctor cannot or does not participate in identification and appropriate helping activities that go far beyond the traditional medical intervention roles, the conspiracy of silence goes on. If private and public ambulatory health care settings (i.e., physician offices, health centers, out-patient clinics, and emergency room clinics) were more skilled at case identification they could be of great assistance in linking the older woman to an appropriate source of counseling. The clergy may also be an important potential service of assistance, but only a few are adequately trained.

What type of clinical intervention might be most beneficial to these women for a majority of these victims? It would involve approaches that would enable the older woman:

1. To make some change in the social and environment context of her victimization;

2. To move beyond the point of self blame and inadequacy;
3. To realize that she is a unique individual and has the right to receive help for her specific problems;
4. To derive interventive assistance that extends beyond the moment of the crisis;
5. To participate in her own problem solving.

Task-centered approaches and behavior interventions with older women victims may have great potential for dealing with the wide range of problems that these older women experience. The availability of qualified individuals to provide intervention with and on behalf of the older women victims of violence is a challenging and realizable goal. These women have the right to help, and fulfillment of this right is a basic first step for helping older and elderly women victims of all forms of violence.

REFERENCES

Blechman, B. Behavior Modification with Women. Unpublished paper, Wesleyan University, Middletown, Connecticut, 1979.

Brot, S.P. Neglected Elderly in Eastern Missouri. Unpublished paper, Missouri Association for the Prevention of Adult Abuse, St. Louis, Missouri, 1979.

Cayley, M.A. Conciliation Counseling in a Family Court. *Federal Probation*, 1976, *30*(4), 27-34.

Cooper, L. Wife Beating—Counselor Training Manual Number Two— Crisis Intervention. A report prepared by the National Organization for Women Domestic Violence Project, Ann Arbor, Michigan, 1976.

Cormican, E.J. Task Centered Approaches with the Elderly. *Social Casework*, 1977, *58*(8), 490-494.

Davis, L.J. & Brody, E.M. Rape and Older Women: A Guide to Prevention and Protection. U.S. Department of Health, Education, and Welfare, National Institute of Mental Health, National Center for the Prevention and Control of Rape, Washington, D.C.: Superintendent of Documents, U.S. Government Printing Office, 1979.

Dierking, B., Brown, M., & Fortune, A. Task Centered Treatment in a Residential Facility for the Elderly: A Clinical Trial. Unpublished paper, George Warren Brown School of Social Work, Washington University in St. Louis, Missouri, 1979.

Fields, M.D. Wife Beating: The Hidden Offense. *New York Law Journal,* 1976, *175*(83), 1-7.

Flynn, J.P. Recent Findings Related to Wife Abuse. *Social Casework,* 1977, *58*(1), 13-20.

Gaguin, D.A. Spouse Abuse—Data From the National Crime Survey. *Victimology,* 1977-1978, *2*(3), 632-643.

Gelles, R.J. Abused Wives: Why Do They Stay. *Journal of Marriage and the Family,* 1976, *38*(4), 659-668.

Gelles, R.J. Power, Sex, and Violence: The Case of Marital Rape. U.S. Department of Health, Education, and Welfare, National Institute of Mental Health, Washington, D.C.: Superintendant of Documents, U.S. Government Printing Office, 1977.

Hooyman, N.R., Rathbone-McCuan, E. and Klingbeil, K. Serving the Vulnerable Elderly: The Detection, Intervention and Prevention of Familial Abuse, *The Urban and Social Change Review,* 1982, *15*(2), 9-14.

Johnson, C., Ferry, J., & Kravitz, M. Spouse Abuse: A Selected Bibliography. United States Department of Justice, Law Enforcement Assistance Administration, National Institute of Law Enforcement and Criminal Justice, Rockville: National Criminal Justice Reference Service, 1978.

King, N.R. and Marvel, M. G. *Issues, Policies, and Programs for Midlife and Older Women.* Washington, D.C.: Center for Women Policy Studies, 1982. (Published Monograph).

Pagelow, M.D. Battered Women—A New Perspective. A paper presented at the International Sociological Association Seminar on Sex Roles, Deviance, and Agents of Social Control, 1977. (Available from National Criminal Justice Reference Service, Box 6000, Rockville, Md. 21201).

Pfouts, J.H. Violent Families: Coping Responses of Abused Wives. *Child Welfare,* 1978, *27*(2), 32-43.

Rathbone-McCuan, E. and Hashimi, J. *Isolated Elders,* Rockville: Aspen Systems Corp., 1982

Rathbone-McCuan, E. and Voyles, B. Case Detection of Abused Elderly Parents, *American Journal of Psychiatry,* 1982, *139*(2), 189-192.

Rathbone-McCuan, E. Elderly Victims of Family Violence and Neglect, *Social Case Work,* 1980, *61*(5), 296-304.

Resick, P. A. Sex-Role Stereotypes and Violence against Women, in *The Stereotyping of Women,* (Eds). V. Frank and E. D. Rothblum, New York: Springer, 1983, 230-256

Scott, P.D. Battered Wives. *British Journal of Psychiatry, 1974, 125*(11), 433.

Steinmetz, S.K. *Cycle of Violence: Assertive, Aggressive, and Abuse Family Interaction.* New York: Praeger Publishers, 1977.

Steinmetz, S.K. The Battered Husband Syndrome. *Victimology,* 1977 *2*(3-4), 499-509.

Straus, M.A. Wife Beating—How Common and Why. *Victimology,* 1977, *2*(3-4), 443-458.

Thomas, E. *Marital Communication and Decision Making: Analysis, Assessment, and Change.* New York: Free Press, 1977.

Uhlenberg, P. Older Women: The Growing Challenge to Design Constructive Roles. *The Gerontologist,* 1979, *19*(3), 236-241.

U.S. Congress, House of Representatives Select Committee on Aging. Elderly Crime Victimization: Local Police Department Crime Prevention Programs. Hearings before the Subcommittee on Housing and Consumer Interests of the Select Committee on Aging, 94th Congress, 2nd Session, April 28, 1976.

Voyles, B. Identification of the Abused, Neglected, and Exploited Elder Workshop. Unpublished paper, George Warren Brown School of Social Work, Washington University, St. Louis, Missouri, 1979. (Mimeographed).

Walker, L. E. *The Battered Woman.* New York: Harper & Row, 1979

Chapter 5

LEGAL ISSUES AFFECTING OLDER WOMEN[1]

Paul S. Nathanson

The legal issues affecting older women are significant for them in particular, but their importance extends to a much broader segment of society. Such issues affect all disenfranchized people in the community whether they are young, old, women, or minorities. Only such a perspective will permit us to rectify some of the problems. As an advocate for older people, and, I hope, an advocate for older women within that category, I well recognize that it is important to select certain aspects of a problem, structure them in a very narrow sense, point out their idiosyncracies, and then proceed with legislators and judges to make the particular case for women or for Blacks, or for older people in general.

One statistic that always comes to mind in attempting to describe how such problems interrelate, is that 80 percent of all single Black

[1]Delivered as a lecture at the Gerontology Institute , Sangamon State University, April 1, 1977 and later transcribed.

women over the age of sixty-five in the United States today live on under $1,800 a year. If you view that fact from various perspectives, it becomes an aging issue; it becomes a women's problem; it becomes a minority problem. It is important that we view these issues, whether problems of the elderly, or problems of women, as part of a larger picture, that of poverty. Admittedly, however, to a large extent, issues of poverty in America can well be described as women's issues.

My primary concern as a lawyer, as a legal services lawyer, really is with poverty issues and how they manifest themselves in the United States today. I am the Director of the National Senior Citizens Law Center which is a legal services corporation-funded back-up center. We used to be funded by OEO, and were part of what in the sixties was the War on Poverty, more aptly described by some as a skirmish which never really got off the ground. Certainly, it was dead during the Nixon years.

It's important for you to know what my biases are. I'm primarily concerned with poverty and the issues that have impact upon poverty or tend to cause poverty and within that purview the problems of older women—primarily poor older women. I am concerned with what makes older women poor, when they didn't experience poverty as middle-aged people.

When I talk about legal issues, that is not such an easy phrase. It's not very easy for the lawyers in my office to understand. I mean something beyond Perry Mason. I have in mind a rather broad definition which includes the interaction between judicial (the courts), legislative, and administrative proceedings. What goes on in each, how they interrelate with social policy questions, makes law a sort of codification of social mores, often outlasting the mores, and creating conflicts. Again, the important thing is to understand that there is a critical interrelation between what courts do, what legislatures do, whether on the federal or the state level, and what administrative agencies do. They all interrelate, and in my discussion, I shall illustrate in concrete terms some of the ways in which this occurs.

Why are women treated differently under the law, or why have they been treated differently under the law—all women, not just older women? In general, why have women been "discriminated against by the law?" Policy makers have viewed women as weaker, and therefore in need of protection. That was at least the rationale for public consumption. Women have to be protected by certain kinds of laws, so that they won't become, for example, bartenders. There are many other such forms of protective legislation which started with an initial good intent, as did child labor laws and women labor laws. It was never taken into consideration that perhaps men ought to be protected from having to work long hours under conditions of drugery. Women, it was presumed, are weaker and need protection. We consider them as filling certain roles in society, which we have to further.

It is not surprising, therefore, that social security was designed in consonance with the clear role that was envisioned for women as homemakers, and thus the various benefits they derive are often through the male worker. As a result, a female worker today under Social Security cannot provide all of the same kinds of benefits for her nonworking spouse as can a male worker.[2] Those provisions exist in the law right now. There was a certain role prescribed for women, and this value judgment worked its way into actual legislation such as the Social Security Act.

My view is that, to a large extent, these were ways of using the law as a means of oppression. It is tantamount to saying that a certain whole segment of this society cannot do a particular kind of a job. In the courts and legislatures, it is not uncommon to hear words pronounced and the arguments made that—"Look, there's a man who needs a job, and, therefore, we really shouldn't allow women to take this kind of a job. He's got a family to support." Such arguments are familiar to all of us. That's the kind of reasoning that ends up formulating what we call protective legislation.

NATIONAL SENIOR CITIZENS LAW CENTER

The National Senior Citizens Law Center is a back-up center. That means that we don't take clients at all, but instead work with all the legal aid programs throughout the country, such as the Land of Lincoln Legal Services Program or the Chicago Legal Aid. There are approximately 3,000 poverty lawers around the country who are

---

[2] There have been some recent modifications in this area.

funded primarily by the Legal Services Corporation Act. They take poor people as clients for no pay.

Legal problems of older persons are principally in the areas of social security, public and private pensions, issues involving nursing home guardianship and involuntary commitment, patients' bill of rights questions, Medicare, and Medicaid. In addition, there are legal issues in the home ownership area. For example, why do most zoning laws prohibit, let's say, three elderly widows from living together in the home that one of them owns and now can't really support? All the government benefit programs, such as food stamps, have a special relevance to the elderly.

If a client walks into a legal aid office, and the attorney in that office really doesn't have time to deal with some of the esoteric points of law that are involved, he or she may call the National Senior Citizens Law Center and ask for assistance. Our assistance can run the gamut from providing pleadings to court documents we've already done or have gotten from a lawyer who filed an identical lawsuit, for use in their present case. We are thus often acting as a clearing house. For example, the lawyer in Illinois can get a copy of the same pleadings that were filed in Florida without having to reinvent the wheel, or, unfortunately, in many instances, especially with the present Supreme Court, reinvent the flat tire.

The clearing-house function can be tremendously important. It's really just a way of providing centralized information. We can by very simple means, not necessarily lawsuits, find out, for example, what the public welfare department or the social security administration in Seattle is doing with respect to missing SSI or social security checks that are not being delivered. They've devised some corner-cutting process by which people can get the money quickly. We can act as an intermediary, and let people know what's going on around the country. Or if there's a bungling procedure that's going on, we can find out about it, and then go to Baltimore and discuss it with the Social Security Administration and advocate with them to change it. They at least consider us as having a feel for what's going on around the country at the field level.

In addition to actually going to court or providing the written materials to help lawyers go to court on behalf of the aged poor, we may well draft legislation. The drafting of legislation could be on a federal or a state level. Since we are a fairly small program, it is primarily on the federal level, although we try to provide assistance to local legal aid programs or statewide legislative programs around the country. In Ohio there is a statewide legal services program. We might provide them with some interesting guardianship legislation which we happen to draft in California. Or we may well testify at a hearing on the state or federal level, making the case, for example, why there ought to be certain legislation, or changes in existing legislation.

In addition, one of the major functions we perform because of the expertise we've been able to assemble, is to testify and comment upon regulations. That's the administrative process. Primarily, let's say HEW would be the agency that would send out regulations affecting the daily lives of poor people in America, and there really aren't many people with the knowledge and the time and resources to sit down and comment on Medicaid regulations. We like to think we've got the background that we can at least come up with a cogent and well-articulated argument on why those regulations, or others, are bad or good. We like to think we provide a viewpoint on the federal level for poor people. In order to do that we have 10 lawyers in Los Angeles, each handling one or two substantive areas. We do have several people who are specifically assigned (and they are not just women) to dealing with special legal problems affecting older women.

In addition we have four attorneys in our Washington, D.C. office, and through that kind of presence we're much more able to exert an impact on the federal level. One of the threshold activities that we perform in that office is to send out a weekly newsletter to all area agencies on aging, all legal services programs, and all state offices on aging. We follow a very simple procedure. We go through the federal register on a daily basis and describe what happened, and inform them as to what hearings are coming up in the following week. In order to be of assistance to advocates of any of these issues, we try to circumvent what usually happens, which is to find out 2 weeks later that there was a hearing held where you should have made a presentation, or that a regulation came out which you should have commented on. One of the major things we try to do is get the information out, although we're not the ones necessarily doing the advocating. We see that the information does get out into the field, and that the people concerned in turn write their congressmen, or the various administrative or legislative bodies involved.

CAUSES OF POVERTY

What are the causes of the poverty of older women? The causes include the economic dependency of women as homemakers plus the inadequate dependents' benefits under such programs as Social Security which do focus on women. In addition, women follow distinctly different work patterns which move them in and out of the labor force, rendering them ineligible for a private pension plan. They may have stayed out for 10 years in order to have children or because the husband moves from one place to another. Further, because of earlier discrimination in jobs, women were forced to work in industries that didn't have private pension plans or had very low wages, and therefore they end up getting low social security benefits. Or they work in industries, or as domestic and migrant workers where it's very difficult to prove that you were ever covered under social security. Consequently, women don't even get social security.

Such patterns result in the availability of very limited resources when you're older, such as a private pension, and, very rarely, a survivor's benefit under a pension plan. Also, there are seldom any savings since women, by and large, had to work in low-paying jobs. The net effect is that of four-fifths of all the single black women, and of half of all the single women in the United States over sixty-five-percent of their number live on under $1,800 a year. It is by no means just a minority issue. Women over the age of sixty-five in America can be said, to a large extent, to be poor. It is a result of earlier discrimination, and ultimately of pension systems that don't accurately reflect the role that we force upon women at an earlier stage. In addition, there is job discrimination. Women can't really find jobs if they are between forty and sixty-five, even though there is legislation to protect people from sex and age discrimination. Specific legislation has little effect, if it's not enforced.

THE DISPLACED HOMEMAKER

I should like to relate a story about the displaced homemaker. I was in a city park about 3 years ago. It was a lovely spring day, and I was sitting on a bench minding my own business when a woman, a very well dressed woman in her mid to late forties, sat down next to me. We started a conversation. She asked me what I did, and I said I was involved with legal services for poor and older people. She conveyed in the course of the conversation that she was a well-respected member of her suburban community. She was very well dressed in a tailored suit. She had three children and confessed to a very comfortable lifestyle. I asked her what she did. Well, she was a prostitute. We got into a lengthy discussion of why she was a prostitute, and the long and short of it was that there was nothing else she could do to earn a living. That is, not to keep her enjoying the lifestyle, or even close to the lifestyle, that had been hers when her husband walked out. She had absolutely no training, and there were no jobs for which she had the requisite skills.

Now this is not a funny story, but actually the scenario of the displaced homemaker. The characteristics in general are as follows: women in their forties or fifties, without children in the home, and not disabled. I'm developing these categories so as to delineate the types of programs that might be made available for women who are usually widowed, or more recently divorced after 19 years of marriage.

This woman was a homemaker without a job, because home was where she was supposed to be, and she really didn't have any training in anything other than being a homemaker. She certainly did not have any recent work experience. She may well have worked and given up that job, because her husband had been transfered. She hadn't, however, worked in the last several years, because she was raising the family. Well, the husband is gone now. The economic realities are something like this. Unless it's a very unusual situation, there isn't any substantial life insurance, assuming that she's been widowed. If it's a divorce, the realities are even more harsh. We have sort of a backlash, wherein women married over 20 years who had bought the American dream find themselves in court and getting divorced. The judges, primarily male, say to these women, "Okay, you want to be independent—terrific. Okay, but no support. Everybody goes out on their own, and everybody deals with their own lives themselves. That's the way you women's libbers wanted it. Right?" It is almost a vindictive situation, totally unresponsive to the facts.

A woman in such a case finds herself all of a sudden at middle age with no support, although she's bought the dream all along. Further, she has no training. The odds are that she doesn't have any substantial savings, so I think we've pretty clearly made the case that she's poor, or close to it. She does not qualify for the Supplemental Security Income Program because that covers the aged, blind, or disabled. Since she's not disabled, and she's not sixty-five, and doesn't have any dependent children living in her home, she qualifies only for general relief which varies from state to state, and within states, from region to region. In parts of California it is possible to receive perhaps $85 or $100 a month, and in some places $10 a month. I'm sure that it varies throughout the country.

She really has no place to go. Her job prospects could be fairly described as pretty dismal. She has no recent work experience. She has no training. There is very well documented discrimination both with respect to looking for work and getting hired, when you have both the age and sex bias against you.

We have laws on the books—Title VII of the Civil Rights Act, on the one hand, the Age Discrimination in Employment Act of 1965, on the other. You'd think an older woman would have a better chance finding a job because we have regulations against both age discrimination and sex discrimination. This is not the case. What we need to learn about the legal process and how it really works, is that having a law on the books does not mean that there is an immediate effect upon people's daily lives. The Age Discrimination in Employment Act has an allocation of $2 to $5 million for enforcement by the Labor Department nationwide. EEOC which enforces the Civil Rights Act is totally overwhelmed.

What results is a game of "hot potatoes." EEOC sends you to Labor, and Labor sends you to EEOC. You go to EEOC and say, "I can't get a job," and they say, "Oh, yes, we know why. It's because of age discrimination, but we don't handle age discrimination. You have to go to the Labor Department." We know what the Labor Department does. "It's not age discrimination; it's obviously sex discrimination. You ought to go to the EEOC.'' The issue is tossed back and forth, and nothing happens.

Not only is there job discrimination for this category of women but there's clear discrimination with respect to training for jobs. There are all kinds of federal programs to train people, such as the WIN Program. However, if you're not male, the odds are that you are not even going to get into one of those. So you are, I think, in a fairly tough situation. It's almost impossible to get credit, and that sort of completes the picture.

The fact is that the woman described earlier is poor; she has no place to go; she has no government benefit programs; she has no insurance left over, and no other source of income. This leaves her in pretty dire straits. Who is she? She's the displaced homemaker.

There aren't any simple answers to these problems. There is the beginning of a movement to do something about it at a threshold level, certainly not in a far-reaching way, and that's what's called the displaced homemaker legislation. NOW has a special task force on older women; the Chairperson is Tish Sommers. The displaced homemaker legislation actually emanated from her office, and where it stands at this writing is as follows.

On the federal level, it has been introduced by Senator Birch Bayh in the Senate and by Yvonne Burke in the House. It had been introduced, but it didn't go anywhere last year. Unless there's a lot of action at the grassroots level, it won't go anywhere this year. It had been introduced last year by Yvonne Burke in the House and Senator Tunney, who no longer is with us, from California.

That's the situation on the federal scene. The legislation has been introduced. California and Maryland have both passed it, and in California now it has been in existence for a year. I don't have any recent data on what's happened with it. Although both states have passed displaced homemaker legislation, Maryland, in addition, has passed legislation to require a certain number of state jobs to be part-time jobs. The whole employment picture is very important to the women's movement, and specifically to older women.

What does the legislation in fact do? Well, it really isn't all that helpful. It doesn't put a lot of dollars in the pockets of these women. It creates centers which do some of the following, optimally all of the following, and, optimally well. They are informed as to job opportunities for women in this category, and they are in touch with job training. Always, of course, because they are going to be centers of, presumably, information and sharing, they may well be the focus for advocacy if something is going wrong. If you get 50 women coming in and saying that ''X'' employer has turned all of us down, by such massive numbers you may well be able to build a better lawsuit or legislative tidal wave. You have all of these women coming into the same center. It's an excellent form of organization, above and beyond what it provides in information with respect to job opportunities and training opportunities.

Such centers also offer psychological counseling. Given the situation in which they find themselves as widowed, divorced, or on their own with no money, there are numerous possible problems which confront those women. It is important that they be informed about the availability of government benefit programs, of certain housing programs, food stamps, and of local government benefits. Furthermore, such information is available in a supportive kind of environment. In addition, money management is another area to which they give consideration. Admittedly, the last of such skills is part of the stereotype, but let's just for a moment not shun the stereotype. There are certain women who have not learned about money management, because as mentioned earlier, they bought the dream prescribed for American women. So at least at these centers they learn how to buy insurance or how to handle financial affairs in general. These are some of the problems of the displaced homemaker.

PRIVATE PENSION PLANS

Private pension plans are an extremely complex area. There are several issues, however, which have a special impact on older women. But by way of background, this is an industry that involves some $200 billion. It is larger than all mutual funds and all insurance funds. Our problem, of course, has been as a legal center for poor people in general to have those funds really opened up, so that they start paying benefits to people they say they're covering. There is some question as to how regulated it is now, but, at least on the surface, there is pension legislation, ERISA—The Employee Income Security Act.

As a personal aside, I am frequently asked how I began to deal with legal problems of old people. I used to be a lawyer for a 200 person law firm in Los Angeles, and I drafted pension plans. I would see the booklets that we designed which had somebody on the cover waving goodby as they left for their trip to Europe. On the back often appeared a picture of a smiling older man going to the mailbox to pick up his check. It doesn't happen. That whole experience made me think about the other side of the issues.

We were lucky at the legal center that we knew a little about pensions so that we could start filing some of the lawsuits. Pension plans as they relate to the nonworking woman, such as the widow, present particular problems. Up until the 1974 legislation, and even after 1974, because a lot of the provisions don't apply yet, if you were dealing with somebody who's already retired, all kinds of waivers and time periods are encountered. For many people there never was such a thing as a mandated joint and survivor option.

What is the joint and survivor option? The covered worker who qualifies can, before retiring at sixty-five, elect to have a pension paid to his wife after his death. What happens with that kind of a provision? First of all, up until the new act, there was no requirement even that that kind of provision be included in pension plans. And, even if there was that provision, it was fairly rare that it was elected. Just given the effects of inflation, the facts are that men, when faced with such choices, say: "Look, do I get a $100 pension, or do I just take single life pension for myself as long as I live, and just hope that I don't die before my wife? Or do I take an $80 pension now, with the joint and survivor option intact?" The family has decided in many cases that they'd take the risk, because that $20 was very important. Unfortunately, probably in plenty of other instances, such conversations never really went on. I doubt if the husband said to his wife, "Look, do you think we ought to take a joint survivor option?" Rather, he just didn't do it. Following his death, the wife shows up at the pension office and says, "He was getting a pension, and I know I was supposed to get something afterwards." And they say, "He didn't elect that option; I'm sorry."

Even worse is the situation which prevailed, and I think still does, in some pension plans. A man worked for thirty years. At age sixty-five he was going to retire. At sixty-four, he elected the joint and survivor option. He thought about it. He was going to take care of his wife, or his widow, should he predecease her. He retired at sixty-five, lived for a year and a half after sixty-five, and then died. His widow went to the pension plan office to take care of the preliminaries, such as a change of address to which to send the check, and was informed by the pension plan administrator, "It's really too bad, because you didn't read the little print over here. It says he's got to live for 2 years after retiring before that option takes effect." There's no justification for that kind of a provision, other than purely preventing people from getting their pensions. In other words, if someone is sick around retirement age, the company is saying, we don't want to let you elect the joint survivor option. We're trying to file a lawsuit to challenge that. It's a very tough case, but that's what goes on.

Then came ERISA, the Employee Retirement Income Security Act of 1974. That legislation requires that all pension plans have a joint and survivor option which provides at least for a survivor benefit of 50 percent of the benefit the male worker would have gotten. You have to have that provision. Now here comes the kicker. The worker can opt out of that. We've shifted the burden, so to speak. In other words, if he doesn't do anything, at least that provision will come into effect: there will be such an option, should he predecease her, and she'll get 50 percent or more, depending on what the plan says.

However, he can opt out of it. And again, given political or economic realities, he may well decide to. What we would like to see, and what does not now exist in the law, is that at least she be able to get notice of the fact that he's doing that. That is just a small part of it. Our impression as lawyers on behalf of the women in these situations is that they are never really finding out about the fact that he's decided to cut her out of even a minimal 50 percent.

So we would like to put a provision in the law. Such minimal provision would mandate that the spouse be notified of the fact that the decision to opt out of the survivor benefit is being made or contemplated. I would go even further, although I think there are constitutional problems, certainly in non-community property states, which is the greater part of the country, in really mandating that she have to sign off, in effect be involved in the decision, or that it be a joint decision. You might be able to do that in community property states where they both have a current right to that pension. You would have real trouble, say in the Midwest or in the rest of the country, with that kind of provision.

One other major problem for the widow in the private pension area is that if the worker dies before retiring, no matter how many years he's worked, except for perhaps a minimal thousand dollar death benefit or something like that, she gets zero.[3] The rationale is that this is, in effect, an insurance program. You play the game; you take the chances. It's said very coldly. If he dies before age sixty-five or whatever the retirement age is, it does not matter how many years he's worked, or that he would be vested.

As an additional illustration, let's say the man has worked the requisite number of years to be vested in the pension plan, 10 or 15 years, depending on which rule they are using, and then he continues to work, and then dies before retirement.—Nothing! Even if he had left the job, the wife still wouldn't get the benefits if he died before retirement. There still is no right to pension. Divorcees are worse off than the widows under discussion, except in community-property states. Now in community-property states, although it's been forgotten by lawyers representing women in divorce actions, the woman does have a right to half of the vested benefit. In other states, in most of them, you get divorced, and his contribution has gone into earning that pensiojn; she has no right to it at all. It's not an asset of the marriage in that sense. That has been the lot of the nonworking woman, with respect to pensions.

Less than 10 percent of single retired women get any kind of a private pension. So private pensions have certainly not been any bonanza for working women. The problems relate again to work patterns, the non-recognition of temporary work, the moving about, really with no say, and taking off 2 or 3 years to have a child which society has built into the prescribed destiny of women.

The new pension law has brought about some changes. It's a little complicated, but it's minimized the problem. Problems still exist in terms of break in service, if a long break is made. In addition, women have worked in industries without pension plans, such as smaller shops, and as domestics. They never ended up covered by a

---

[3] Unless the plan provides for early retirement and certain elections are made.

pension plan, or even given the chance to work long enough to qualify. Even where they did work, because of earlier discrimination and unequal pay for equal work, they get lower pensions because the pensions, as social security, are based on the dollars they earn. So it's a vicious cycle.

The use of sex-based actuarial tables is to provide, in effect, lower pensions to women, or to require higher payments by women, into a pension plan in order to get equal benefits at the time of retirement. That's what goes on with TIAA-CREF, which is in the university pension system. This issue is currently being attacked by several lawsuits in the Equal Employment Opportunity Commission.

Let's look at the people who design pension plan provisions. They sit around a table (usually men smoking big cigars), and they decide that they want to provide the workers in an industry a $100 a month pension. They then have to figure that out in a very complicated way. They have to know what kind of workers are in the particular industry; what's the rate of turnover; how often they leave; as well as other related characteristics.

In the past they have focused on the characteristic that women tend to live longer than men, and, therefore, if a particular industry is to pay a woman a pension of $100 a month, the odds are, it would have to be paid to her over a longer period of time. Therefore, it's going to cost the company, whoever's funding the pension plan, more dollars when they go to the insurance company to have a $100 a month pension for a woman, than it is to have it for a man. Therefore, the decision is: we are going to do one of two things. We are either going to require that the woman pay more money into the contributory plan than the man, or we're going to pay her a lower pension. We'll pay her $90 a month, given that she may live longer—in other words, the actuarial equivalence. The thing really to remember is that what they're doing is treating women as a class, and using life expectancy tables to determine that they get a lower pension. That's the end result.

No one wonders why those same life expectancy tables don't crop up when we're talking about mandatory retirement for everybody at age sixty-five. You might argue that women live longer, so give them a few more years to work; or why have other kinds of characteristics never been folded into the actuarial studies used to fund pension plans? Probably, I imagine, smokers, as a group do not live as long as nonsmokers. I would imagine that they, in fact, ought to get a higher pension, because they are not going to live as long. Or they should pay less into the pension plan. Also, Blacks should be getting a higher pension earlier. That's been argued by some people with respect to Social Security.

If you're going to use actuarial tables for different groups, why just women? There's some good news on the horizon. A case called Manhart vs. City of Los Angeles[4] recently affirmed in the Ninth Circuit Court of Appeals, a 1976 case, was just decided at the end of the year. A municipal retirement plan which required 15 percent greater contributions from women than men was held to violate the Civil Rights Act, Title VII, of the Civil Rights Act. They ruled that each person within the plan had to be treated as an individual. It is the same issue as in age discrimination; it's the same issue when you talk at the other end of the spectrum, about youth. We are finally trying to deal with people as individuals, with individual characteristics, rather than grouping them all together. That's what the court said in the Manhart case. You cannot use sex-based actuarial tables to decide that you are going to exact a greater contribution from women.

In addition, there's an Oregon case, a State Court case, which ruled that it's a violation of the Civil Rights Act to provide different-sized (lower) pensions to women than to men on sex-based actuarial tables. The issue is very much in the courts right now.

SOCIAL SECURITY

Special hearings were held last year by the Senate Special Committee on Aging on women and Social Security. They had a task force study and hearings in which people from a variety of backgrounds testified on different angles of Social Security. There are obvious problems in the Social Security Act which involve clear sex discrimination. In other words, certain benefits are provided to the female spouses of male workers, again based on the old theory that the worker was probably going to be the man, and the woman would be

[4] Approved by the United States Supreme Court.

in the home. She was getting a certain kind of a benefit, but the male spouses, the nonworking male spouses of female workers, do not get the same benefits. It is clear that the work of women is valued less. In other words, if you work a year as a woman, your work covered by social security employment doesn't earn you the same kinds of benefits for your family, or your spouse, as would a man working the same year.

That was successfully challenged in the U.S. Supreme Court. I think it is going to be successfully challenged in other instances, such as that of Wiesenfeld vs. Weinberger. In the Wiesenfeld case a widower with children in his custody challenged the provision of the Social Security Act which did not give him the same social security benefits it gave a widow with children in her custody. He was in exactly the same situation. He just happened to have been a non-working spouse. His wife worked. She died, and he wanted the same social security benefits that she could have gotten had he been the worker. It had to go all the way to the U.S. Supreme Court, and he won. The court said that it was unconstitutional to devalue the work of women.

At the hearing I observed a couple of fascinating sidelights. I sat next to Wiesenfeld and we talked. He told me, "You know I won that case, and I think it's been 6 or 9 months already, and I'm not in the computer yet." What that says about the legal process is that winning a case doesn't amount to a hill of beans. We've already seen that having a great piece of legislation doesn't mean too much, unless it's effectively enforced. Winning a major lawsuit doesn't mean a lot, unless it's effectively enforced either. And here is the direct plaintif in a U.S. Supreme Court case still not in the computer, still not getting the benefits he's supposed to get. Imagine the situation of similarly situated men, widowers, around the country who never heard of Wiesenfeld. I can't picture people going out to the Social Security Administration and informing them of their new right to get a pension. That's the first lesson that I had from those hearings about the legal process.

The second part was that the senators, most of them lawyers, who were involved in the hearing were saying, "O.K., that's really great." Everybody else was complaining about other sex-based kinds of discrimination in social security. They said, "That's really terrific. The courts are going to take care of that, and therefore, we can direct our attentions to another area within social security. We don't have to worry about those obvious discrimination provisions." That's interesting for a couple of reasons. One, you see the legislative branch abdicating some of its lawmaking power because it thinks the courts are going to take care of the situation. Perhaps more significantly, you see the legislators not aware of a Supreme Court decision—that's the judicial branch, which had come after Wiesenfeld was decided; but before these hearings. A decision called *Salfi* severely limited the procedure by which you could even take that kind of case on appeal. In other words, Wiesenfeld could not have been brought after Salfi; but you have legislators, the legislative branch, not really aware of what the judicial branch is doing.

For example, we had a case in San Francisco, the Oliver Case, challenging the fact that divorced husbands cannot get the same kind of a pension benefits as can divorced wives. That case was thrown right out of the court after Salfi.

The major point I'd like to make now in regard to Social Security is that homemaking is not a covered kind of employment, for all kinds of bizarre reasons that you hear very reasonable men enunciating. "Well, how do you tell when somebody retires?" "How much is homemaking worth?" We are capable of sending someone to the moon, but we can't ascribe a dollar value to how much homemaking is worth! Various studies have been done and figures varying between $4,000 to $8,000 have been set as the value of what homemakers do.

One alternative that I should like to suggest is this. If you happen to have a situation with two families who are friends, living next door to each other or in close proximity, you might well try this just for fun. It's sort of a classic switch, but just for homemaking purposes: have Mr. A's wife—assuming he's working outside the home—have him send his wife next door to Mr. B as a domestic. Mr. B would then pay social security and take it out of her wages, and she would pay social security. Have Mr. B send his wife over to Mr. A's house to do the shopping, housecleaning, whatever. They would both be covered in their own right under social security. Well, that's a bizarre solution.

Marriage, under the Frazer Plan, is considered a partnership, and the spouse working at home really helps the spouse who is working at a job to earn the dollars that the job worker is earning.

They each have a right to a part of those dollars, and each have a right to their own social security benefit based on those dollars. So in the proposed system, they would credit each spouse with their own social security accounts, in one of two ways. Fifty percent of the couple's combined earnings, in covered employment, would go to each of their accounts, to the woman and the man, if both worked. Or if only one worked, and this is the primary situation, where only the man is working, 75 percent of the worker's salary would be credited to each account. As a result, the man would have a social security benefit based on 75 percent of his earnings. The wife would have a social security benefit based on 75 percent of his earnings. This would be her *own* benefit.

In addition to these specific kinds of legal problems that affect women and older women, there are general legal problems of the poor that—I think a good case can be made—apply to a majority of women or have a specifically strong impact on women, because of their economic situation. Although in a certain sense they are general legal problems, age discrimination and mandatory retirement are factors that affect all parts of the aging community, but can be said to have perhaps special impact on women. This is particularly the case for a displaced homemaker who has grown older, and needs the work, but doesn't have very high social security benefits. She wants to continue working, and then is faced with mandatory retirement. As I said earlier, one might advance the argument that since women are supposed to have a longer life expectancy, maybe they ought to work a few more years—although I would shy away from presenting that argument because I don't like to see it used as a basis. Or maybe we want to approach the problem from the standpoint that everybody has a fixed number of years to work, and, therefore, if women are in and out of the work force for 10 years to do the society's work and take care of children, maybe they ought to be able to retire at age seventy-five.

I think there are all kinds of permutations that we could talk about, for example, the area of civil commitment and guardianship. Although, again it's a general legal problem, because women may be more apt to live alone and have no one else to help them, it may affect women more severely. The courts, having a certain view of the helpless women who can't manage money affairs, etc., etc., may be more likely to proceed with guardianship or civil commitment kinds of cases. So the whole due process issue which we've been working on in terms of having a right to a hearing, becomes very important for old people in general, but, I think, specifically for older women.

It's amazing to me that if you're fifty years old or twenty-five years old, and you want to go out and spend all of your money on red balloons, nobody cares. As soon as you reach sixty-five or seventy, and you want to go out and spend all your money on red balloons, there's suddenly a number of people around who care. You're regarded as kicking up your heels, and you're acting silly. Therefore, we ought to have a guardianship declared over you—not because we're worried about what you're doing, but because we're worried you're spending our money. And we're your kids.

We did an interesting study in Los Angeles. In the guardianship and involuntary commitment proceedings some possible limitations on very substantial rights are occurring, such as the right to determine where you live, the right to manage your own money, and the right to avoid being put into a nursing home, in effect, or into some other institution. These substantial rights are being adjudicated, and in less than 2 percent of the cases are the people represented by independent counsel—not necessarily a lawyer, but some independent advocate. When you combine that with a study recently done in Ohio which showed a .942 correlation between being represented at these kinds of hearings and not being institutionalized and not having a guardianship declared, you start to see the significance of representation at these kinds of hearings. The U.S. Supreme Court has held several years ago that juveniles in juvenile proceedings have a right to independent appointed counsel. It does not yet exist for guardianship proceedings. A majority of civil commitment and guardianship statutes in the country still provide that you can have that proceeding go on without being represented by your own counsel, without being present at the hearing, and without even having actual notice of it. It's all designed on the theory that we all know what's good for mama—including the daughter who wants to live in mama's house.

The Supplemental Security Income program is the basic national welfare program for aged, blind, and disabled categories. Within that program they have a feature called the six month rule. The design is this: if you're an individual in a certain state, you get

$200 as your benefit, if you qualify for SSI. If you are a couple you may get $300. In other words, two can, as we all know, live cheaper than one. So the government has decided instead of giving you the two individual benefits, it will give a reduced couple's benefit. If two people are married or presenting themselves to the community as man and wife, they get a reduced benefit; they get a couple's grant, which is less than two individual grants.

There is some humor in all of this when you read the SSI claims manual, which is the manual used for the local district offices to understand and interpret the statutes. Because the government will end up paying less dollars, if they can prove you to be a couple—only $300 instead of $400 in our fictitious state—they really try to have you be a couple. All of a sudden the government is in the business of legitimizing relationships. So without telling the individuals when they walk in the door why, they ask the couple a whole list of questions to aid the detective worker in getting these people to be married or representing themselves as such. They ask, "How do you introduce each other at parties?" "How are your names put on the mailbox?" This is done without explaining why they are trying to prove they are a couple. I would imagine a lot of older people, even if they weren't really living together full-time or had at least some possible argument they weren't representing themselves as a couple, would probably try to legitimize the relationship and say, yes, we're married or we live together. They would probably say we're married.

Unfortunately, what happens if, let's say the male leaves the home, and they are getting a couple's grant: there is this wonderful device known as the sixth month rule. This means that for a period of 6 months, even though he's gone and she's living alone, they will be presumed to be a couple. What social security says is we will take half of the couple's grant and send it to wherever he is, and we'll take the wife's grant and send it to her. Now that sounds rather fair, because they both get $150, instead of $200, for a period of 6 months.

It's not all that simple, because usually the couple, and probably the man, has an extra asset. Let's say they were getting a social security benefit and he was getting a small private pension, enough to be substantial but not preclude their getting SSI, because it's a need-based program. Let's say they qualified for their couple's grant of $300, and he got a pension of $100. Therefore they were only entitled to a $200 SSI benefit; $300 is the full couple's grant. They had independent income which was his, social security, or a pension check of $100. You subtract that from $300 and you've got a couple's grant of $200. Well, that's fine, I guess.

You get $300 to live on while they are both living together. Now he leaves. Now he gets his pension or social security check sent to him, plus half of their $200 benefit. He's living on $200, and she's still getting half of their $200 benefit; she's getting $100, because you'd better believe she's not seeing half of his pension or social security check. Now that happens for 6 months. That's the present law.

Another provision which I think has a particular impact on women, older women, is that if you go into a health care institution for a full calendar month or longer, you get a reduced, $25 SSI benefit. You only get $25 to buy whatever you want while you're there. This really perpetuates the person's institutionalization. Say they are only there a short period—for two months. Two months of $25 income, on the incomes most of these people live on, would probably mean that they would lose their apartment or their home, because they have no way of meeting the payments for it. So where is she going to go when she gets out? Obviously, she stays in the institution for the rest of her life.

There are numerous other legal issues affecting women which call for discussion. Those touched upon here are sufficient to indicate the broad perspective required to properly assess and to act upon them.

Chapter 6

INSTITUTIONALIZED WOMEN
Some Classic Types, Some Common Problems and Some Partial Solutions

Nancy Mayer Knapp

Few people make a free choice to live in board-and-care or skilled nursing facilities, yet placement there is frequently for an extended period of time and probably for the final segment of a person's life. The following discussion is about the increasingly large number of older women in these institutions. They have commonalities with aging women in other types of institutions, including acute care facilities, hospices, state hospitals, prisons, single room occupancy hotels, and even convents, but each of these smaller groups has additional characteristics and needs which are not the focus here.

To help understand some of the classic problems of older women in institutions, we will look at some arbitrary categories. They are very arbitrary, but unfortunately there are many precedents for using arbitrary categories in institutions. When we attempt to accommodate complex behavioral symptoms and problems, we seek helpful generalizations, some of which may become stereotyped. Our prime concern is the person, but paradoxically, a single aspect of our concern may become almost the whole person in our frame of reference

— for nurses there may be a fracture or impaction in room 8, dieticians differentiate between their low sodiums and their blands, business office staff uses funding jargon so that a person may become a Medicare, a private, an SSI or a DPA, student interns eagerly request actor-outers or hallucinators. Each of these labels represents our selective point of view, and at best, a service oriented goal; however, depersonalization is implicit in the process of labeling.

Depersonalization is one of the worst by-products of institutionalization, and so the arbitrary categories used here come with a sort of 'consumer warning.' They are presented as convenient classifications to lead to fuller understanding of women in institutions. Each generalization should elicit not only examples of people who fit within the category, but examples of people who are the exceptions to the generalization. Each labeled category is an assemblage representing real people and actual experiences, but presented with the knowledge that real people are far too complicated to be put into our study-mill and extruded packaged like geriatric Barbie dolls. For each category we will look at general characteristics, specific examples, speculations about etiology, and some appropriate therapeutic techniques and responses for their symptoms.

The usefulness of the categories is that they are, like real people, admixtures of many different characteristics familiar to almost every institution. In most cases these institutionalized women have counterparts in institutionalized men. Although few human characteristics are confined to either sex, male and female roles frequently differ in board-and-care and nursing facilities. For a well known variety of reasons, most geriatric facilities have a majority of females among both residents and staff. On the other hand, most facility owners, administrators, medical doctors, and physical therapists in these settings are male, a continuation of a lifelong sex stereotype of authority figures for most of this generation's elderly. This tradition influences nearly all of the types of institutionalized women whom we will discuss.

Basic human characteristics also know no racial exclusiveness. The people in this discussion could belong to any racial or religious group, but it is significant that women who are also members of minority groups and who maintain that numerical standing in institutional placement, are in multiple jeopardy. Their minority status, superimposed on whatever individual problems exist, deserves particular awareness from the staff. A Black woman who has never been exposed to white people, or who has known them only from a servile position has her reasons to dread placement in a primarily white facility. The Chicana matriarch whose world evolved around her family and home life, may find it especially wrenching to be alone in an Anglo setting, as will the Asian woman who has difficulty understanding English and has acquired no taste for meat and potatoes. A Jewish woman who has been oriented toward her children and religious pride may feel singularly 'cast out in her old age.'

Geriatric staff must have an understanding of reasons for identifiable cultural behavior and expectations, and they must be sensitive in demonstrating that they value these traditions. A visit from a Black Gospel Choir, a party patterned after a Mexican fiesta, travel slides of China followed by tea and fortune cookies or a morning baking bagels, may all sound like cliches, but they represent legitimate program activities, readily available for geriatric facilities, and possessing twofold potential to prevent alienation and to develop pride.

Because many early emigrants were eager to become assimilated, older people often do not know much about their motherlands. It can be a gift for them to learn about the costumes, customs, foods, and other characteristics which match up with their surnames. The facility as well as the individual will be richer as a result of exposure to cultural variety which provides a good antidote for the institutional tendency toward uniformity.

Figure 1 represents the first of the specific categories of institutionalized women for our study. She portrays the territorial terrors of the geriatric world. She no longer performs her main role in life whether it was as a homemaker or a fashion designer. She no longer has her family, she no longer has her home, and she no longer has her health. What she does have is a specific chair in the front hall, and God forbid that anyone else should sit in it. She may even be territorial enough to fight off trespassers with a cane.

This is the same process described by Robert Ardley in *The Territorial Imperative*. She is seeking to differentiate herself from the rest of the home. She has acquired her rank or status by occupying the chair, and that is going to be her resting place. It is the niche for

Figure 1

her to achieve her identity and the only way that she can avoid being anonymous in this great group of anonymous people.

Other women may stake out their territory in an elevator or at a card table in a public room where free access should be assumed. Less primitive manifestations of the same process are seen with women who begin by being very helpful in some aspect of the institutional operation. Commonly the craft program needs someone who is adept at cutting patterns, sing-a-longs often need an old pro at the piano, and the receptionist welcomes someone with whom to share a late night cigarette, and to answer the telephone when she goes to the bathroom.

Initially these roles may be positive for the resident and may not impair any group function. But what happens when the visiting doctor is not allowed to get into the elevator, or a visiting family is verbally abused because they inadvertently sat at 'someone's' table? What happens if the helper in the craft room gradually extends her position into preventing other people from helping, or covertly or overtly discourages other people's attendance? What happens if the piano player devalues the singing of enthusiastic, but off-key residents, or refuses to let someone dance 'because she'll make a fool of herself'? What happens when the receptionist's helper gossips about personal or administrative business or looks through mail and other confidential material?

Part of supervisory duty is to monitor similar interactions in a way to encourage positive individual roles and responsibilities which can provide for one person's territorial needs without impinging upon another's. A network of basic policies and a tone set by therapeutic procedures and emphasized in in-service training can help prevent and respond to problems related to territorial issues. Additionally it will acquaint paraprofessional staff with an understanding of related dynamics, including how to react when falsely accused by confused and paranoid patients.

Provisions for as much individual territory as possible is good preventive practice. The nature of board-and-care allows for more personalized dominion than a skilled nursing facility can provide, possibly including private rooms and keys for doors, drawers, and mail boxes. The paucity of possessions in both settings may increase their importance to residents, especially to a woman whose identity has been closely tied to previous home environment and to tangible items such as fashionable clothing. Accurate inventory of personal articles and a reasonable acceptance of the responsibility for them would help to minimize the petty thievery and careless loss or destruction of personal property which is painfully common in institutions. Shoddy laundry service is not the least of the problems, since, for a woman who owns very little, a nice robe may represent a significant part of her world. Care in marking, sorting, washing, and distributing laundry may not be trivial issues for an institutionalized woman, but they are routines which can be controlled in a well-run facility. Provisions for able women to do their personal laundry is beneficial and can easily be incorporated into therapeutic goals with other activities of daily living.

One basic territorial symbol of our identity is our personal name. It costs an institution nothing to make a big point of using not only the appropriate, but the preferred names of patients, both visually and verbally. At times it is desirable to have them on doors, beds, dining chairs, and other personal space. The charge of every staff member from administrator through maintenance person, should be to learn names and to use them frequently. *Granny* or *Honey* are not acceptable substitutes. Attention should be given to the proper pronunciation and spelling of unusual and foreign names. Introductions of one resident to another as well as to new staff members should be a continuous process; it is a reinforcement of her importance as an individual. The origin of names and the meaning behind them is a good topic for talk groups and general sharing. One very negative woman demonstrated a remarkable change in her attitude when she discovered in one such group that her name meant 'Helper of Mankind.' Exercises and games to help memorize names are as important as exercises which maintain muscles. Song fests which spotlight people's names are great reinforcers of positive identification. Among others, we have known several *Amy's* whose day was made by hearing *Once in Love with Amy,* and a very regressed and withdrawn Suzy whose rare moments of awareness were stimulated by hearing *If You Knew Suzy.*

If a woman has been married several times, but prefers to restore either her maiden name or favorite husband's name, she shoud be allowed this. If her social security check comes in a name which she prefers not to use, the business office can be flexible enough to conduct their business with one name and extend to her the courtesy of using her preferred name, or they may help her apply the proper documentation to have her social security account name officially changed.

Territorial issues are frequently very hot between roommates. As much as possible they should be encouraged to work things out as adults, but it must be acknowledged frankly that it is very difficult to share so much of your life with someone whom you may not know well or may actively dislike. Intervention and tactful mediation may be a major part of staff function, but clearly established policy about standard issues such as the use of television and bathroom facilities, alternate places to read or view TV late at night, and designated equal provisions for personal possessions and entertaining visitors, are helpful preventive measures, which address issues rather than personalities.

Much behavior in institutions is predictable, but there should be an open approach and individual assessment of specific instances. One woman who seemed to be a 'typical territorial chair squatter' was in reality waiting anxiously for her 'son, the Doctor.' She had missed one of his treasured visits, and subsequently waiting for him became a full-time occupation, an undesirable situation for both mother and son. Staff and family collaborated to encourage a change. She promised to go to certain activities, he promised to seek her there, and staff promised to keep both informed about the other's whereabouts in the facility.

A major responsibility for geriatric staff is to help people discover appropriate and satisfying roles and territory. A person who is happy with her own world is less likely to need a slice from the world of someone else.

The lady in figure 2 is probably familiar to everyone. In an extreme of territorial excess she is a hoarder, and maybe even a kleptomaniac. She surrounds herself with countless things which are of at least fleeting importance to her. It is almost inevitable that she will have a clash with the staff or with a neater roommate. It is Housekeeping's task to keep the institution neat, it is her task to keep it full. The dining room staff has a task to keep track of their utensils; her task is to help herself to what she might need. Nursing has the task to keep her neat and healthy; she has the task to rummage through not so neat and healthy trash.

Figure 2

Fortunately, an inveterate collector within an institution will have some limits because of finite storage, but many manage to stretch that by carrying vast quantities with them at all times. A staff person who develops good rapport with her might utilize her saving ways by having her collect things for specific craft projects, or justify her natural proclivities by getting her involved with a purposeful community recycling project.

Attentive prevention would have been the best action for the hoarder in one facility who gathered 31½ sets of dentures one night and put them in her pillow case like the ultimate offering to the tooth fairy.

As always, it is important to investigate the reason for the symptom. In the course of a regular room check, one alert woman was discovered to have a huge horde of paper napkins. These were confiscated, both to her shame and fury. She tearfully threatened suicide, and the reason for her collection finally emerged. She had a physical condition causing a continuous dribble of urine. Nursing staff was unaware that she had a problem, because following her habits of more than eighty-nine years, she took care of her own needs. In her customarily frugal and efficient way, she would go through the dining room and take unused or slightly used napkins and make herself utilitarian pads. She flatly stated, "I cannot afford sanitary napkins; I cannot afford rubber pants." It did not occur to her that it would be appropriate for someone in the institution to provide directly for her need. The intimacy and trust for sharing this type of problem in an institutional setting must be cultivated.

Figure 3 represents any of a number of very hostile women within nursing home settings who conduct a reign of terror which serves to protect themselves from any close relationship with either staff or other patients. Their maladaptive techniques are so carefully hewn that their efficiency dazzles.

Hostility sometimes manifests itself in the form of physical abuse. Many places have powerful sluggers or pinchers, most of whom have intensely sad histories which partially explain their problems. One woman had literally been abandoned at a nursing home. She had gone there regularly to play the piano as a volunteer, and was taken there for a 'weekend' with her suitcase. The weekend turned out to be forever, and her family disappeared. When she realized

Figure 3

what had happened, she destroyed her beautiful wardrobe, including a mink coat, and retired to hospital gowns. She never touched the piano again, but she did become an elective mute and a selective pincher. When she walked down the hall, several people would give obligatory shouts of "Look out, she'll pinch you!" and then she would provide the obligatory pinch. It must have given her a transcendent rush of power for one instant.

Some people in similar situations punish themselves with abusive self-stimulation, as did one woman continuously hitting herself and singing "Iris is a bad girl, Iris had a baby, Iris is a bad girl." Whatever form it takes, raw misery is a very wearing phenomenon for staff to cope with, including chronic complaining, swearing, and other verbal abuse. When readily available remedies such as ignoring, selective re-teaching, distraction by involvement in other activities, displacement or diffusion of energies, rational discussions, attention to problem-solving details, and other approaches do not work, a new point of view or outside help may be invaluable.

The coincidence of the introduction of a new mental health program with a crisis of one patient's acting out, helped the patient significantly, and gave the program credibility. The patient was one of many in nursing home settings whose suicide attempts resulted not in death, but irreparable damage. She had been an attractive, fairly successful singer, married, and a mother. In a rage precipitated by a fight with her husband, she had shot herself. The resulting spine injury left her helpless, but young and physically strong enough that she would be likely to live in that condition for many years. Her main form of communication became random screams or inappropriate sexual remarks. Her beautiful face had become contorted, and her voice had become abrasive. Many of the staff members were justifiably tired of her abuse and convinced that she should be in a state mental hospital.

Simultaneously, several events occurred which served as an intervention for this woman. An intensive program was brought into the facility from a local mental health center. Because of her high profile and the general awareness of her problems, she was an ideal prospect to work with. There was not a person in the nursing home who had not heard her scream; to cut down on the number of screams would be a gift for everyone, and a process of which all would be aware. A diluted form of behavior modification was organized in which she was permitted an activity or visitor(s) of her choice, but would be cut off from them immediately if she screamed. A beauty school student was recruited as a volunteer to work with her hair and nails. And, also, because her teeth had completely deteriorated during prolonged periods of tube feeding, the Department of Public Assistance arranged for dentures which simultaneously improved her nutrition, speech, and appearance. A fortuitous event occurred at the beginning of these intense activities. She deliberately made a terrible mess with syrup on her breakfast tray. The cook became furious at the waste of food and the needless cleanup for her staff. She stormed into the woman's bedroom to express her anger, but as she did, there also was a wonderful spark of transference, or understanding, or affinity between the two, and the cook, a warm and wise person, became, in effect, the woman's prime therapist.

As in the case of the cook, it is a great gift in an institution for the entire staff to be directly involved in the therapeutic team. It is not unusual, in this type of standard routine, for the cleaning woman to spend just as much time with a patient as a nurse would spend. She should know the patient's name and be encouraged to talk a little. She should also have the freedom to report to the supervisor any changes which she notices. Such involvement is well established in institutions which practice milieu therapy, and dividends accrue in both improved patient care and increased staff satisfaction.

With particularly hostile patients, the facility is stronger if it uses a network of community resources and specialists to supplement its staff. Volunteers and student interns are also important additions to personal contact so that a patient does not have to act abusive in order to receive attention.

Another commonly institutionalized woman who needs special backup is represented in Figure 4. She may think of herself as an aristocrat, or a successful person. Her orientation assumes that she will have a dignified, self-suffiicent existence. She has always prided herself in her composure, poise, and correctness, but this entire life style has suddenly been stripped away from her because of an absolutely overwhelming medical problem. It is probably the first time in her life that she has been confronted with a problem for which there is no solution. She may try to ignore the fact that her identity is now tied

Figure 4

up with a diagnosis such as multiple sclerosis, or muscular dystrophy, or hemiplegia, but she is confronted with ugly reminders of it everywhere because she is in a health care facility. Her body betrayed her and left her with an unnatural assortment of objects such as bedpans, wheelchairs, tubes, and hypodermic needles.

Frequently such patients need help in nurturing a reason to continue living. One alert but physically devastated woman was anchored to her wheelchair. She was introduced to a crisis-line program for which she could actually work as a volunteer. With the aid of a dialing device on her telephone in the nursing home, she had a regular group of 'at risk' people whom she called daily. Of the many people whom she helped in this manner, none knew of her condition; for them, and for her, her functioning mind and her empathy were her most important qualities.

At times, 'prescriptive pampering' may help people who feel selectively discriminated against by their diseases. One effective response to a group of patients with cerebral palsy, sharing quarters in the same wing of a facility primarily housing much older patients, was made by their local chapter of United Cerebral Palsy. They collected funds designated to hire a special aide in addition to regular nursing home employees. She was hired to provide special services which might include playing a game, carefully laundering a delicate sweater, writing a note or listening to daydreams, all functions which could be regular provisions in a perfect institution, but which would never take priority in an average institutional schedule. This additional care provided something special, and appropriate.

It is important to supply all of the information patients desire about their own diseases. The facts may be bad, but their conjury in imagination is probably worse. Seminars for patients regarding specific health topics, films combined with discussions led by nurses or doctors, or panels of other patients with similar diseases, have had excellent results.

One of the most common problems in institutions is diabetes, and one of the most common complaints is institutional food. These two elements combine to present a loaded situation for the diabetic. She may be in the institution because of her inability to regulate her condition properly at home. Commonly, she feels cheated, and, therefore, she justifies cheating a little herself. It is usually helpful to have people with similiar dietary restrictions eat together. Special compensatory treats such as relish dishes and ingenious efforts to find appealing substitutes for the forbidden treats, as well as special expressions of interest and support from the dietician, help the diabetic person feel more indulged than deprived.

Regular 'programming can be adjusted for people with acute problems. A non-verbal person should not be excluded from verbal groups. One spunky Indian-Irish woman could not speak as a result of a stroke, but she wrote messages on a magic slate which the group leader read to the group. Her pithy comments on politics were treasured and repeated throughout the facility. Another person with throat paralysis would whisper remarks to the leader who would repeat them to the group. This encouraged others to risk more because they knew that they would also be helped and that all comments were valued.

Frequently, simple devices are not adequately used to simplify physical problems. Adaptations of eating and other self-help tools are valuable. Positioning yourself to facilitate eye contact with wheel chair patients and posting notices for their eye level lessens their strain.

The person in Figure 5 represents the frail and dying people within the institution. Nearly everyone's first choice would be to die in her own home, in her own bed, and surrounded by the people and things that she loves best. Unfortunately, this does not always happen.

Most current literature treats dying as a developmental stage, with the quality of preparation for death depending upon the quality of mastery in previous developmental stages. Since the pioneering of Elizabeth Kubler-Ross there are many books, seminars, and programs available for people working with dying patients and for the dying themselves. Suddenly death has become a very important process, with many theories, some of which are contradictory. Two guidelines appear to be universally encouraged. These are: to avoid hypocrisy and to treat death as a natural part of the process of living.

For the patient there are many groups, including volunteers, who specialize in sensitive support for the needs of the dying. The best of them are very good indeed.

For the survivors, it is important that the staff be professional in all aspects surrounding death. Some families wish to be present when

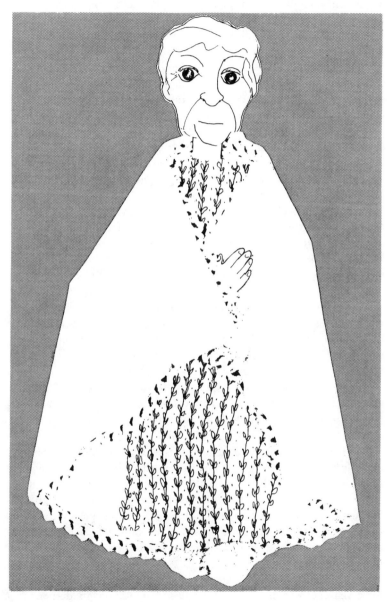

Figure 5

death is imminent, and many nurses experienced in geriatric work have almost uncanny instincts to interpret patterns and to anticipate when this will occur. Details for notification of death and for handling personal property should be well established to minimize stress.

For patients, it is important to handle information of another patient's death in a forthright manner and to allow for grief and mourning among them. Sharing the difficult news with roommates, table companions, and special friends before rumors circulate is important. Simple, dignified, memorial services may be provided in the institution, since attendance at funerals is often impractical.

Special need exists for a supportive network of staff to provide both appropriate resolution of personal grief and to prevent burnout. Most professionals agree that there should be a limit to the number of dying people with whom anyone works intensely at a given time. This may vary according to what is going on in a professional's personal life at any given time. No matter how professional or experienced we are, we cannot, and actually should not, work continuously with people without sometimes feeling somewhat unprofessionally involved.

The lady in Figure 6 is familiar in most institutions. Her way of dealing with her problems right now is to isolate herself from the world, and she has skillfully built a wall. Her defense and coping mechanisms should be well respected. She may be gruff, aloof, and sometimes hardly civil. Her life has probably required her to be very independent, and it is likely to be important to maintain some vestige of this independence. Life may also not have allowed much frivolity and waste. It is demeaning to her to try to coerce her into making pipe-cleaner flowers, and she probably would not be caught dead with a playing card in her hand.

Whatever her background, her life is likely to contain a history of many losses. If she is from Europe, she may have been affected by the Holocaust and other horrors. If she is from the Midwest, she may have been exposed to other forms of harsh personal realities. Frequently we do not know the histories of many people with whom we work in intimate circumstances, and we must habitually respect the limitations and personal preferences of their involvement or noninvolvement.

One prototype for this category was invited regularly to activities for 2 years. It was always a matter-of-fact invitation, made person-

Figure 6

ally, but with a concerted effort not to take the unanticipated refusal personally. Suddenly, one day she showed up at a talk group. No one knew for sure why *then*, and why for that activity, but it happened that she gradually changed in a way which no one could have anticipated. Not only did she attend some community programs, but she testified at a hearing on problems of the aged. She spoke so eloquently that she was asked to do some televised spots for the United Way. She became a bit of a celebrity and thrived on her new prominence.

It would be wonderful to set a formula to produce such changes. Frequently the best we can do is to be accepting of people at whatever stage they are, offer dignified options for change, and be available when they are ready to exercise those options.

Figure 7 is a woman who is dealing with the present by living in the past. She is probably confabulating because her earlier life, especially in perspective, is much more interesting than her current life. She is an illustration of the disengagement process which was once considered inevitable. She is coping with her life in a way which for her provides personal comfort, but which engenders general discomfort for people around her. When she says, "My husband is going to pick me up; he would never allow me to stay in a place like this." It may be debatable whether to look her in the eye and say, "Your husband has been dead 30 years," or to say, "Well, come into the activity room until he arrives." Neither of these responses show much ingenuity.

Appropriate responses depend, among other things, upon the stability of the person and your relationship to her. One alternative is to use the opening of the reference to her husband to allow her to talk about him. If you say, "Tell me about your husband." She may simply ignore the request, or she may jump at the opportunity. The tense of a reply may be significant. "He *was* very wonderful," indicates that she recognizes that he is gone, and she may be eager to reminisce about him. If she says, "He's on a secret mission for Immanuel Kant," she may be living with an elaborate delusional system.

One of the best techniques for working with people who are living in the past is to provide a legitimate outlet for their symptoms. Making ice cream with a hand-crank machine, or butter with an old churn, triggers recollections of good and bad times, and puts them in a context about which they are likely to know far more than the younger staff members working with them. Revitalizing their experi-

Figure 7

ences is a good vehicle for gathering diagnostic information, and our interest enhances their own valuation of their backgrounds.

A woman in one facility was very isolated because she spoke only an obscure Scandinavian dialect and had no family. She did nothing but sit and stare. One day she spotted and grabbed some carding tools and wool which had been brought for a display. She used them with the vigor of a young girl and with the skill of a professional. It was only a momentary episode, but it was a valuable discovery of something which might be built upon.

Many geriatric institutions include people who are there not because of problems limited to the aging process, but because nursing home or board-and-care placement in the community is considered a less restrictive surrounding than a state hospital. Because of their chronicity they may have much in common with more elderly residents, but because of their relative youth and possibly bizarre speech patterns or appearance, they may be frightening to the older patients and their families. A woman who greets visitors with the patter of a madam from a bordello and who refers to other residents as her ladies, may be either annoying or amusing, but she probably needs to relate to people and only knows how to do this by being crazy.

In facilities with active reality-orientation programs, confused patients may be trained to give correct answers or to avoid threatening topics, but much conditioning of that type is only marginally useful compared with the effort required to effect it. Learning the names of roommates and aides is far more pertinent than learning the name of the person who is president of the United States. The reality that is most important for them is their own, not ours.

The woman in Figure 8 is having a different sort of hallucination for different reasons. These may be drug-induced and related to stress from recent medical problems and loss. She is walking in a peculiar manner because of what is going on in her head. It may appear that the ceiling is coming down, or that the floor is going up. It may seem that her legs are stumps which she can hardly move.

One maiden lady of seventy-five had worked as a bookkeeper and took great pride in the control of her life, much as she controlled the numbers on the ledgers she kept. Everything was orderly, predictable, and perfect for scrutiny. She had been able to continue working

Figure 8

as an accountant in her home past her retirement age, another sign that she was in control—"unlike other people who had to go out to pasture at 65." Suddenly she was forced to have a colostomy, a process which she found disgusting. She had no family or close friends, and had managed not to need them. Suddenly she was plummeted from a life where she had everything under control to a point where she had absolutely no locus of control. Even her body and her mind seemed to have assumed wills of their own. She had frightening stories to tell staff, other residents, and random visitors about people in her room chopping up furniture, who would next chop up *her*. Sometimes reality conspires with fantasy to make things worse. One paranoid woman had her television stolen from her nursing home room while she was already in the throes of delusional persecutions. Many people who fear that they are being poisoned reinforce their fears with newspaper headlines and TV specials on pollution.

One of the first places to start with a person in this condition is with a complete medical checkup, performed with empathy and explanations, and followed by well-regulated checks on medications and reactions to them. Frequently a person who is going through an episode of this type may become normalized mentally, taught to live with her physical condition, and be able to live in a board-and-care or nursing home for many years. A measured reaction to problems of this sort can avoid a premature placement in a locked facility or state hospital.

The wonderful little lady who thinks she has bugs under her skin, may in reality have a skin problem which needs to be treated. The person who feels that she is unfairly possessed by demons because she has always been a Republican and an Episcopalian, probably is feeling unfairly treated for other reasons. Although their complaints may sound amusing, the function of their misery is not designed to divert the late night staff. Training should include firm guidelines never to feed hallucinations. It is possible to empathize with a person who is bothered by frightening fantasy, recognize how real they are to her, but maintain the fact that you do not see them also. Role-playing is a good device for practice of techniques so that the staff may gain feeling for what a patient experiences in such situations, and to gauge possible appropriate responses when a situation is frightening, or unnerving, or seems funny.

The only thing less welcome in the world of nursing homes than a 'dirty old man' is the 'dirty old lady' in Figure 9. Like many of the women in this series, she exists. Therefore, she deserves, and may intensely need, the staffs time, respect, and understanding. We might like to modify the way she dresses, but that is none of our business. She may embarrass us by seeming promiscuous, but the fact that she is a consenting adult makes that none of our business. What does become our business is to be available if she seeks our counsel and, by our own measured response and matter-of-fact attitudes toward sex, work to temper the reaction of other residents, sometimes other staff members and family.

Stereotypical responses to her forthright libido might start with "She's too old," or "It's too bad she can't have a long-term relationship with one man." Her ability and determination to fulfill her needs may be keen enough that she may be involved in a series of heterosexual, bisexual and homosexual alliances. She may in fact be all talk and no action. Socialization at the senior center dances or participation in other activities outside of the institution walls could provide appropriate outlets for her energies which are generally social, as well as sexual. At the very least, provisions can be made so that she need not be reduced to carrying on in the linen closet.

Married couples in nursing homes frequently are not accorded the privacy which they should be able to take for granted. Couples who meet, court, and marry while in institutions are fortunate, and should not be subjected to snide remarks and roadblocks. Intimacy is so frequently lacking in institutions that it should be nurtured wherever it appears.

Institutional responses to romance vary surprisingly. One facility sent the police after a couple who eloped to a motel; yet another actually paid for a motel room for a couple since there was no better alternative to offer. Ethics, physical health, mental health, religion, family pride, financial inheritance, and institutional reputations are some of the complex factors affecting policies and decisions regarding sexual practices. The primary consideration is that love is not just for the young and the beautiful.

General sex education is an appropriate function for an institution to fulfill. Facts are desired about topics which were not openly discussed a generation ago. Questions regarding homosexuality,

Figure 9

masturbaion, and pornography frequently come up, even in groups such as current-events discussions. Many elderly people have shown impressive flexibility in adjusting to changes in their grandchildren's life styles compared to their own. They frequently demonstrate more openness and willingness to grow than some younger people.

Sexual information should be part of the orientation for young and inexperienced aides, to minimize awkwardness of prudish put-downs or giggling embarrassment. Policies are better not based upon arbitrary 'rights' and 'wrongs' from rigid religious or moral codes, but the weighing of such values as 'comforting or harmful,' 'consent-ing or forced,' and 'constructive or destructive.' Institutions may contort our perspective so that the normal seems abnormal, and the aberrant becomes standard. Sex, it should be remembered, is normal.

Nearly every facility has some manifestation of the symbiotic couple. It may be as in figure 10, an aging mother and her, not quite so aging, forty-nine year-old little girl. Usually the mother will be very domineering, following her lifelong role, and possibly in full enjoyment of lifelong ill health. She may be both protective and manipulative of the daughter who may be functionally, but not actually, retarded. The only hope for the daughter to move closer to the mainstream may appear at the time of the death of the mother, when the daughter may begin day time placement in a sheltered workshop and experience a positive, if delayed, individualization.

Symbiotic relationships may prevail with married couples, sib-lings or long-term roommates. Intervention should be exercised care-fully, honoring the standards and needs of the partners, not ours. In one instance, identical twins of fifty-five, who had been institutiona-lized since birth, were separated and placed miles apart, because one was mean and domineering over the other. Not surprisingly, when the balance was shattered and they each had to adjust to new facilities without the support system of the other, they became grief-stricken and disoriented. Ultimately, their desperation was so conspicuous that they were placed together again. They taught many professionals a lesson about homeostasis.

Figure 11 represents the young old, probably institutionalized as a result of alcohol or prescription drug abuse. She may have other re-

Figure 10

Figure 11

cent health problems and be suffering from a combination of adjustments from retirement to the empty nest syndrome.

Her needs are likely to be quite different from others in the facility. She could easily be 25 years younger than the average resident, a factor which probably complicates an already intense depression. For the social service designee, this woman represents the penultimate opportunity to ply her trade. There is an opportunity to investigate and possibly use almost every social agency available. This lady might be a prospect for the Retired Senior Volunteer Program, or tutoring at a nearby school, or foster-grandparenting at Head Start, or joining the Sisterhood at the temple, or a study group at the church, or a class in adult education. There is an opportunity to make discharge plans that could be realized.

She has justifiable reasons for feeling misplaced in a geriatric facility, but alienation is a common problem in most board-and-care or nursing facilities. Institutional life is not what most people are conditioned for; therefore, a continuing effort is imperative to insure the flexibility of programs and policy, that expectations be individualized, and that, when realistic, goals be upwardly mobile. The hope is that the front door is not one-way, but revolving. People will always be coming in, but some may walk out again.

The woman in figure 12 is obviously confused. Nearly every geriatric institution has patients who wear their underwear on the outside, and other clothing in a seemingly ingenius combination of upside down, inside out and bottoms for tops. This might be a result of chronic brain syndrome or a number of other baffling brain processing problems. Once she is properly dressed, it is likely that she will look very normal and may be able to function quite well in situations which do not demand judgmental choices. Left alone, she may take her clothing off again and replace them in her own way. Staff has several choices of preventive action, such as, simplifying wardrobes and keeping her otherwise occupied, or retraining her in some selective portions of her routine.

Modification of the environment may be one of the most effective controls. If she persists in picking through a floral arrangement, making a mess, wearing the vase for a hat, and it happens more than once, staff has more difficulty learning than she does. (Decorations don't need to be eliminated; they should be hung or placed out of easy

Figure 12

reach.) If full pitchers of liquid, medicine trays, or other inviting hazards are within her reach, that is a staff error, not hers.

A person with this type of dysfunction may maintain long-term social reflexes which are so intact that she could easily join a group at the country club for lunch. There is a canny compensatory process which seems to enable some people with severe problems to recognize that something is wrong, and yet to limit their exposure so that they are able to sustain a veneer of normalcy.

One of these ladies had been in the Miss America pageant, and she still possessed the figure, poise, and general demeanor that had served her so well in that role. She was now suffering from a brain disease of unknown origin and unable to perform most self-care tasks, or to communicate. Her appearance was normal, healthy, and attractive, which increased the likelihood of unrealistic expectations for her, and the awkwardness of her inability. An effort was made to keep her with people where she could be sociable, but encounter no demands other than being pleasant. She could not be shaped to fit routine, but her routine, her clothing, and her immediate environment could be shaped to fit her.

At times there are temporary conditions with similar manifestations. One board-and-care resident had been a licensed clinical social worker. She proudly shared plaques and other tangible forms of recognition which she had earned; she also had a lovely wardrobe and was very careful about her grooming. She was admitted to a hospital for a mastectomy and returned to the board-and-care facility completely disoriented. This was not anticipated. On her first morning home, she appeared in the dining room wearing her prosthesis on the outside of her designer dress. She simply was unable to accommodate the numerous changes which had taken place for her. Because of a supportive group of friends to serve as her advocates, a staff which took some extra time, and flexibility in the institution, she was allowed a period of observation before another precipitous move was forced upon her. A particular challenge here was to help residents exercise their most charitable qualities in the frightening presence of someone else's deterioration.

Not all people are equally susceptible to ravages of institutional living. Some residents and some staff are able to withstand the erosion of spirit which frequently occurs. Figure 13 represents three

Figure 13

women who stand out as archetypes for survival. They are in geriatric facilities because they need regular support services and periodically require some specific attention. They come equipped with a kind of categorical imperative to be independent. These women participated in their decisions to move into the institutions mainly because it represented relative independence, compared to alternatives available to them which generally would have required cooperation, services, and dependency of family and friends.

Of these three representatives of survivors, one had never married, one had been widowed for 50 years, and one had been divorced for 40. The first was inherently cheerful with an accepting, generous and optimistic disposition; the second was stubborn, with a feisty, fist-waving temperament; and the third had an exceptionally active mind and an intellectual curiosity which kept her interested in the world. All three had a good understanding of themselves and were accustomed to doing what had to be done.

One needed staff to take the initiative to discover why she always scurried to her room when she was invited to activities. (Her size made her uncomfortable in standard chairs; more suitable seating could be tactfully provided). The second lady needed staff to recognize that her table-mates were repelled by eating with her, and to investigate why. (She used a fork to pick her teeth because they were falling apart—and no wonder, after 92 years of gnashing them. She would not complain about the pain, but once the problem was discovered, dental care could be arranged.) The third needed staff understanding that geriatric programming must be more than nonstop Bingo. (It was also appropriate for staff to facilitate her contact with community resources and with other residents having similar interests.)

All three of these women had some personality traits which might be better modified, but their patterns had developed over many decades and had served them fairly well. Staff does well to recognize lifelong defense mechanisms as such, and to be realistic about expectations, of one adult to another. The survivors do well to recognize that they can receive help within the institutional setting, and still maintain their independence.

Figure 14 represents the greatest challenge to all of us who work within institutions. Maintenance of status quo for a geriatric patient

Figure 14

is, in actual fact, progress. When a patient is admitted, she may appear to be relatively normal. She may be depressed, and she has probably had some sort of recent medical problem and possibly is recently widowed. She may even have moved into the facility to be with her husband during his terminal illness. She is likely to have had pride in life, long respectability, and by her own conformity, probably befitting her generation's sex role, she was likely to be accepting of authority. For that reason, part of our charge is that we not allow her to become overly dependent. She has probably also cultivated the habit of not complaining, and, therefore, we must not allow her to get lost in the shuffle of more demanding patients. It is critical that we not force her to act crazy, or become sick to get our attention.

This is a person for whom old contacts should be encouraged. She should also continue any patterns, such as going to her religious and club groups in the community, to ensure some feelings of continuity and normalcy. She should also be encouraged to start new hobbies or classes. If she can cope with the initial adjustment in the nursing home and live through a first year, she may benefit from a long and stable life in a protected environment.

The women whom we have just glimpsed have had a variety of needs and have a wide range of experience. Each of them, and each new patient, presents a new opportunity for staff to exercise preventive as well as curative skills to prove that life in an institutional setting has potential for growth and creativity. We must not let patients abdicate their responsibility for their lives, and we must not abdicate the responsibility of helping institutions to grow to fit people.

Chapter 7

THE "BABUSHKA" OR OLDER WOMAN IN SOVIET SOCIETY*

Gari Lesnoff-Caravaglia

The Soviet Union, in the eyes of the Soviets, is a developing or emerging nation. Past history is largely discounted, and the Soviets look upon their current state as having been born out of the 1917 Revolution and as being only some sixty years of age.

As a newly emerging nation, the Soviets feel that many of the problems which beset their country are due primarily to its youth. Soviets make constant reference to the fact that things are better than they were, and that they will unquestionably improve even more in the future.

Out of this framework have developed the Soviet attitudes toward aging and older women. The older generation is regarded as having participated in a prior degenerate culture, and is thereby a disadvantaged group.

The Soviet Union covers a wide geographical area, and has some 250 million inhabitants. 11.8 percent of whom are age sixty and over.

*Research sponsored by the Fogarty International Center under the US/USSR Agreement for Technical and Scientific Cooperation.

127

Females account for 52 percent of the population. In the Soviet Union statistics regarding older persons begin at age sixty, as the retirement age is sixty for men and fifty-five for women. But there exist a number of variations in retirement age, and these variations are related to the job profile or the kind of work activity in which the individual is engaged.

Although the Soviet Union regards itself as an emerging nation, this does not mean that all vestiges of the old culture have totally disappeared. Many aspects have been redefined and sometimes reshaped to meet particular current needs and interests. Some features of Soviet life bear strong resemblance to the past—in both positive and negative instances.

A plurality of cultures is much in evidence in the 15 Soviet republics which function autonomously in much the same fashion as do the states within the United States. In some of the republics, one or more totally different language is spoken, with the Russian language appearing as the official or second language. One such example is Soviet Georgia. The elderly, those in the category of the long living and those living in principally rural areas, in many instances do not understand nor speak Russian, and Soviet gerontologists in communicating with them must make use of interpreters.

The Soviet Union has long applied a series of age classifications in studying the elderly population. In the Soviet Union the categorization is as follows:

Zrosli (Mature)	60–74
Starii (Old)	75–89
Dolgozichili (Long living)	90+

Attitudes toward the older Soviet woman or *babushka* were documented during a month-long visit to the western north-central portion of the Soviet Union and the Republic of Georgia. Interviews were conducted with 50 men and 50 women drawn from both the *sloozaschie* or professional/civil-service class and the *rabochie* or working class—the two major social class distinctions in the Soviet Union.

Areas considered in this study included general attitudes towards older women, sex roles, work opportunities, educational opportunities, familial expectations, and societal norms.

General Attitudes Toward Older Women

There was total agreement among those interviewed (100 percent) that older women were revered in the Soviet Union. The respect paid to older women was in part related to the fact that they were responsible for the rebuilding of the nation following the great Patriotic War (World War II). Respondents also made frequent reference to the fact that older women had lived under tyranny of the Czars, had endured inequities of every description, and had been deprived of medical care and educational opportunities.

Institutionalization of older persons was regarded by the total group with repugnance, particularly with respect to their own kin. Several persons replied with indignation: "Why, no one would do that. We do not place our elderly relatives in institutions."

Such responses were given further documentation through visits to nursing homes in which the same responses were given by directors and personnel. The staff of nursing homes said they felt particularly obligated to provide the best of care to older women who came to live in these homes because their entrance into such homes was predicated upon the absence of living relatives. Relatives would be caring for such older persons, it was generally felt, if they had not given their lives in the war or died as a result of it. The majority of the *guests* in nursing homes were female.

Older women thus are looked upon as *invalids* of the war, or war veterans. As veterans they are eligible for all benefits accorded to this group by the state, including priority for medical care (both inpatient and outpatient), prosthetic devices, beds in nursing home facilities, and places in health resorts.

Sex Roles

Although women participate as equals with men in all levels and phases of work, it is still the practice for women to assume major responsibility for the care of the home and children, with the husband playing a secondary role. His main function, when there are children, is to assist the children with their schoolwork.

There is some disagreement among respondents as to the extent to which such role expectations functioned, but there was much agreement (87 percent) that the appropriate role for the woman as she grew older was that of the *babushka* or granny. In 20 percent of the responses there was some qualification that it might be appropriate for the grandmother to continue her career, but that if her help was needed in the home of a child, it would be more appropriate for her to take on the role of *babushka*.

Those respondents (30 percent) who did not have a babushka in their home, said they regretted the situation. Comments that could be interpreted as negative or somewhat disapproving of the older woman's continuing her work career were voiced by 45 percent of the respondents.

Older professional women continuing to work in positions of responsibility, such as division chiefs or laboratory heads, were regarded with mixed feelings. Those who had achieved prominence in their fields were regarded by 70 percent of the respondents as rightfully continuing a successful career. The remaining 30 percent expressed views that ranged from resentment at their occupying positions which blocked promotion possibilities for younger people, to responses which indicated that there was some question of an older person's capacity to function optimally in such demanding positions, to statements which indicated that older women frequently served only as titular heads. Older men in similar situations were regarded more positively by 88 percent of the respondents.

Positions of great responsibility (Directors, Managers, Heads or Chiefs) were, in general, held by men. This is particularly true in the medical profession. While 75 percent of the physicians are women, the majority of these physicians hold only the Candidate of Medicine designation. The title of Doctor of Medicine is given generally to men who have distinguished themselves in their careers or have gained international acclaim. Although it was frequently reiterated that such opportunities were not closed to women, the face remains that more men than women achieve this goal.

Work Opportunities

Soviet citizens have the option of continuing to work following retirement, or to accept their pension and become veteran workers.

The state encourages older persons to continue working because of the severe labor shortage. Approximately 50 percent of the Veteran Workers continue working after retirement.

Women, upon reaching age fifty-five, or retirement age, frequently choose not to work. This decision is based usually on one of the following reasons:

1. They feel that they have fulfilled their obligation to the state;
2. because of ill health; or
3. in order to help their children at home.

There is a recent gradual increase in the number of women who continue working after reaching retirement age. Reasons given for this change included:

1. a challenging career or position;
2. preferring the salary to the reduced retirement benefits; and
3. unwillingness to surrender the apartment which was included as part of the work arrangement.

The government's recognition of this change in preference on the part of older women has been in part responsible for the recent introduction of a new child-care regulation. Women are now permitted to remain at home with a newborn infant for 1 year with full salary. Although child care centers are available, many are overcrowded, and parents without *babushkas* are hard pressed to find proper caretakers for young infants. This new regulation has also been described as part of the national preventive health program to insure the development of healthy persons who will continue to be productive until advanced old age. The Soviet scientific interest in the longliving of Georgia is also an expression of the national concern in having people live long and productive lives to offset labor shortages.

Not only does the retirement age for men and women differ, but there is an additional difference in retirement age based on the type of work performed by the individual. There is a branch of Soviet gerontology, Gerohygiene, which concerns itself with the assessment or profile of each job or position in terms of stresses experienced at particular ages. In such assessments biological changes are also taken into consideration. The profile of the position and the profile of the individual are matched. When there is a match in terms of observed stress, the person is offered another less strenuous job. In this aspect, a person can experience several work careers, but these shifts appear to be more in a downward direction.

Older professional women may continue in their same posts at the same salary when reaching retirement age. Older working women, however, who wish to continue to work are usually graded downwards, although a fair number continue to work at their same jobs until their health begins to fail. Older women who work as wardrobe mistresses in theatres and museums had often held clerical positions before reaching retirement age; janitresses become doorkeepers; and those in less skilled jobs often become street cleaners. On occasion, older women were seen begging in churchyards.

When questioned about this flexible system of retirement, respondents were unanimously in favor of it. Criticism of the system was offered by 22 percent of the respondents with respect to who made the decision as to when the person should be moved to a different position or job, as well as some questioning with regard to the fairness of some of the decisions invoked. There was no feeling that women were discriminated against in such a flexible ordering of work opportunities, although 18 percent indicated that job profiles tend to indicate one sex or the other because of the nature of the work.

Educational Opportunities

There are almost no educational opportunities for older women. There are some programs in a few cities on educating older persons to the processes of aging, physical fitness groups, clubs for pensioners, and health resorts which offer recreational activities.

Older women do not then return to formal learning situations, nor is there provision for second or multiple careers through training or education.

When questioned as to the need for such education and training, respondents were interested in the possibility, but found difficulty in assessing its usefulness. The concept was one outside their orientation toward work in the Soviet Union. If ever instituted, 15 percent felt that it held less application for older women, as older women preferred the *babushka* role to any other.

Familial Expectations

The average Soviet family is small in size and consists of one or two children; a family of three or four children is considered large. Respondents gave as reasons for the small family size: work style of family members (both parents working); housing shortages; the materialistic ambitions of the family, and the widespread use of birth control measures and abortion.

The presence of the grandmother in the home of a young family is not unusual, and very much desired. The acceptance of the *babushka* in the three or four generational homes is based upon a number of factors, among which figure prominently the expectation that one takes care of one's aging family members, along with the general reverence for the aged.

Maintaining an older person in the home is more easily accomplished because physicians make house calls, and in some regions a visiting nurse and social worker, as well as a variety of community services, are available.

Respondents had no hesitancy in describing the advantages of having a *babushka* in the home. The *babushka* is *the* baby-sitter in the Soviet Union, as there is virtually no domestic help available. The *babushka* allows the young couple freedom in conducting their personal lives and careers and from much of the druggery of housekeeping. Care of the children, responsibility for the daily shopping — which means standing for hours in line for each commodity you wish to purchase—and general housekeeping are often tasks assumed by the *babushka* and are regarded as acceptable ways of relating to the family of her child— usually a daughter.

The *babushka* may move in with the family, or not, as she prefers. It is to the family's advantage to have her move in with them for a number of reasons. All of the grandmothers, having worked, receive a pension. This pension, along with free public medical care, makes the *babushka* independent of the family in financial terms. In fact, many grandparents provide financial assistance to their mature children.

Further, the allocation of apartments—and most urban populations live in apartments—is based upon a number of square meters per person. Accepting the grandmother into the home means that the family can apply for a larger apartment, as the grandmother has a right to a room of her own.

The benefits to the grandmother are also great. She has a meaningful role to play within the family and society, and she continues to live within the warmth of the family environment. Her needs are met—she is usually respected by the son-in-law and adored by the grandchildren whom she, in turn, spoils.

All respondents gave examples of mutual benefits to be enjoyed; 29 percent stated unequivocally that this was the most fulfilling role for an older woman.

Societal Norms

In response as to how older women were regarded differently from older men, 87 percent replied that there were no differences; both groups worked as long as they wished or were able; both would be cared for by family members should the need arise. Older married men were regarded by 88 percent as being properly cared for by the elderly wife, while 62 percent thought it proper for the aged husband to care for his ailing aged wife. Other relatives and hospitals were mentioned more frequently in connection with older women.

Most respondents appeared to have difficulty with the concept of retiring as a time when one did not contribute to society. It was expected, in their thinking, that older women would continue to work as long as possible, either in the *babushka* role or in holding a position or job outside the home. Although pensioner clubs do exist, they are not widespread. They had difficulty in grasping amusement or recreation as possibly the sole activity of the older woman upon retirement.

There is genuine attachment to older female relatives. Special reverence is accorded women because they had rebuilt the nation following the Great Patriotic War in which 20 million persons perished, the majority of whom were men. In the aftermath of the war, women filled positions traditionally occupied by men and continue to do so to this day.

March 8th is set aside as a national holiday to celebrate the contribution of women to Soviet society. Gifts, greeting cards, and a national holiday mark this day, which includes, of course, the honoring of older women.

It is expected that older women will retain religious sentiments and will attend church services. This is described by 39 percent of the respondents as something resembling a weakness. Most of the churches, however, do have men in attendance, although the worshipers are predominantly older women. The role of *babushka* also affords the older woman the opportunity to impart religious training to her grandchildren. Having been baptized in the church through the efforts of the *babushka* was reported by 79 percent of the respondents.

SUMMARY

Results of the interviews with 100 persons drawn from both the professional/civil service class and the working class indicate that the older woman is positively regarded in the role of *babushka* or granny. Less positive evaluations were made of the role of the older woman in more career oriented or professional roles.

Findings also revealed that although economic circumstances (a severe labor shortage) provide older women with greater latitude in work opportunities, male/female distinctions were common. There was little change in role for older professional women, while women from the working classes, upon retirement at age fifty-five, were often relegated to more menial tasks.

Since many of the problems which older women face are the same as those faced by the general population, such as shortage of housing; lack of consumer goods; food shortages; drab, routine existences; dictates from an ubiquitous authority; inability to relocate at will; and a general low standard of living, older women are not singled out as a particularly deprived group. Older women participate in Soviet society on a par with the rest of the citizens.

REFERENCES

Benet, S. *Abkhasians: The Long-Living People of the Caucasus.* New York: Holt, Rinehart & Winston, Inc., 1974.

Chebotarev, D.R. *The Main Problems of Soviet Gerontology.* Materials for the IX International Congress of Gerontologists, Kiev, 1972.

_____. & N.N. Sachuk. Sociomedical Examination of Longevous People in the USSR. *Journal of Gerontology* 1964, *19*, 435-439.

Leaf, A. Every Day is a Gift When You Are Over 100. *National Geographic,* 1973, *143*, 83-118.

_____. *Youth in Old Age.* New York: McGraw-Hill Book Co., 1975.

McKain, W.C. The Family and the Older Person in the Soviet Union. In Smith, T.L. & Man Singh Das. *Sociocultural Change Since 1950.* New Delhi: Vikas Publishing House, 1970, pp. 262-272.

_____. Na Obshchestvennikh Nachalakh. *The Gerontologist,* 1973, *13*, 248-250.

_____. Observations on Old Age in the Soviet Union, *The Gerontologist,* 1967, *7*, 41-43.

Pitskhelauri, G.Z. *The Longliving of Soviet Georgia.* Sabchota Sakartevelo, Tbilisi, 1976.

Quinn, J.R. *Anato   of East-West Cooperation.* Fogarty International Center for Advanced Study in the Health Sciences, Washington, D.C.: 1969.

_____. *Fundamental Principles of Health Legislation of the USSR.* Fogarty International Center for Advanced Study in the Health Sciences: Washington, D.C., 1971.

_____. *Soviet Medical Research Priorities for the Seventies.* DHEW Publication No. (NIH) 74-422.

Storey, P. B. *The Soviet Feldsher as a Physician's Assistant.* DHEW Publication No. (NIH) 72-58, February, 1972.

Chapter 8

WIDOWHOOD
The Last Stage in Wifedom

Gari Lesnoff-Caravaglia

The subordinate role that sexism has delegated to women in general, and older women in particular, in carrying out the role of wife, has made it extremely difficult for women to cope with a crisis which increasingly is becoming a life experience. As more people live long enough to reach the age of sixty-five or beyond, more women, because of the fact that they do live longer, experience the state of widowhood. There are approximately 9 million widows in the United States to date.

Ill prepared as many women are to take responsibility for the direction of their lives, on an economic, financial, and psychological level, among others, women find that once their spouses have died, that they enter a foreign world. Fifty-six out of every 100 women becomes a widow. This figure is three times that for men to become widowers. The longevity of women is one contributing factor to the increase in the number of widows, but there is also the fact that in our society it is the custom for women to marry men who are at least several years older than they. The result is that not only does the woman, by natural circumstance, outlive her husband, but the fact that the husband is older when they marry, serves to insure the probability that the wife will survive him.

At the present time there is no provision in our society for women to prepare for the role of widow. We do not willingly engage in discussions of death, nor do we have specific ritual or mourning procedures for the widow to follow. Mourning, as a practice, is on the decline, and those who face bereavement do not know how to assume this role or what behaviors to adopt. The grief the widow experiences is real. She cannot deny her emotions, nor the psychological and often physical distress which accompanies this event. Yet she cannot turn to society for assistance, nor look to friends for support, nor even rely upon her own family.

What compounds the entire problem is that while the widow is experiencing her greatest moments of grief and distress, she is expected, minimally, to take on the responsibility of arranging for a funeral, and to assess her financial situation. In other words, while she is under major psychological stress, she must at the same time make practical, emotionally disturbing decisions in regard to where she intends to live, what to do about the deceased spouse's clothing and possessions, and how she is going to handle the new roles thrust upon her.

It is not surprising that there is a close connection between the experience of bereavement and the increased need for psychiatric and medical attention. This is particularly true if we consider that the relationship, especially among some older couples, may have taken on something of a symbiotic quality. When one partner dies, life loses meaning for the surviving spouse, and death may ensue shortly afterwards. Severe depression may also result, leading to acts of suicide.

Because the experience of death of a close relative or friend is encountered in our society about only once within a period of 20 years, death is very much a stranger to many people. Because death is so seldom met, it takes on a mysterious and frightening aspect. The consequence is that persons who face death, or who experience the death of a close relative such as husband, are often ostracized by former friends and associates. It is as though the survivors have been tainted. There is the further expectancy that within 3 days, once the funeral is over, everything should resume its everyday aspect. In other words, there should be no reminder or sign of death. When there is, even by way of mourning and references to the dead, the bereaved person is avoided.

Furthermore, the death of someone whom we have known well or for a long period of time arouses feelings of anxiety about our own death. If the death was of a person over sixty-five, the friends and relatives may wish to deny the death even more, because not only is there the reminder of death, but in such instances there is the added reminder of old age. Along with our denial of death, we wish to deny that we age.

The adverse effects of the death of an older person are also experienced by adult children, at the death of a parent. The surviving parent then stands in a different relation to his children. If it is the mother who survives, she may be regarded by the children as childish or irresponsible. An older son may feel he has to take on the role of the deceased father as a counselor or advisor. If she doesn't follow his advice, this may cause a rift in the family. The widow is sometimes perceived by the children as a burden.

What the widow discovers, also, is that in seeking comfort from relatives and friends, they do not know how to respond to her needs. She hesitates to ask someone to help her work through her grief, as she fears to become a bother or senses that intimacy based upon death is not welcomed. As a result, the widow must mourn alone. Some women become "perpetual" widows—like monuments in cemeteries—simply because they are unable to resolve their grief.

Once the widow is ready to re-enter society, she may find it less easy and smooth than she may have anticipated. We have developed a societal pattern of couples, and are uneasy about accepting a single woman into our social circles. This is particularly difficult when the woman was accepted into the circle initially as part of a couple. In her new role as widow, she appears fragmented, or in some way peculiarly splintered off. To overcome the discomfort the widow occasions by her presence, friends may hasten to provide a dinner partner, a date, or escort. The anxiety betrayed by such a response to a widow demonstrates the need to deny death. Her presence thus becomes a reminder of the unspeakable.

Part of her sense of entering a foreign state or a new world—in much a Kafka-like dimension—is due to the widow's lack of understanding of what the mourning process entails. Her ability to cope with her own feelings, or new sets of feelings, can be enhanced and strengthened, if she knows something about what happens to persons who grieve. The widow is bombarded with conflicting, unusual emotions, the need to make decisions, and the inability to determine what to expect of other people, along with not knowing what to expect or is expected of herself. Many women have the sensation of becoming an entirely different person while attempting to resolve their grief. Frequent and unrestrained weeping at unexpected moments, is one example, especially when the person is not customarily given to expressing her emotions in such a fashion.

There is a great deal of pain associated with grief. We ordinarily expect a person who has experienced the loss of a limb or who has undergone major surgery, to feel pain. We also expect such persons to be somewhat incapacitated because of their painful experience. Yet grief, which is among the most painful of human experiences, passes unrecognized. Such pain is intensified by this lack of understanding, and occurrences of every day, such as the delivery of mail, or the newspaper, is regarded by the bereaved person as symbolic of the world's indifference or total lack of interest in her suffering. It is an insult that life can continue much as before, and not take notice of the changes wrought in her personal life.

The lack of self-understanding as a grieving person, and the differences which the widow perceives in herself, are frequently causes for alarm. Many widows, because they did not know what to expect, fear that the strange new self they have become is the result of mental deterioration—or insanity. Even the lethargy that often accompanies grief comes as a shock. The inability to plan for the future, the wish to remain inactive, are all frightening new dimensions of her self.

The bereaved woman is expected to adjust to the demands of society—to stow away her grief. In her wish to become accepted, to reach friendship and rapport as quickly as possible, the widow may conform to societal demands at the expense of her own grief-work. A widow does not usually realize that she needs time—time to practice living without the person who played such a significant role in her life. Further, although no relationship is perfect, in life there was always the opportunity for a second chance, the new opportunity. The finality of death precludes such gestures and the widow needs time to accept this as a fact. Even the acceptance that words like "we" and "us" no longer hold the same meaning brings on personal anguish.

Although within the memory of many people today, death and funerals were a part of home life, death today has been effectively institutionalized. Most people die in an institution of some sort whether a hospital or nursing home or the like. Once the person dies, he/she is sent to still another institution—the mortuary. The family does not learn to live with illness, grief, and death as a natural life sequence. Consequently, the family is unable to provide the warmth and support which are needed in times of crisis. Further, many families have been divided by divorce and remarriage. The likelihood of intimate family relationships is diminished. And yet, the person who mourns needs to be near people who love her and who share her grief.

The widow, further, has to fight a battle against sexism. She needs to understand that part of the reason she feels as bewildered as she does, and that she is so hesitant in taking over the reins of her own life, is that society has relegated her to an inferior status. Her confusion is not due totally to her personal weakness or inadequacy, but at least in part to society's attitudes toward women in general. One reason why she has difficulty in making decisions is that she has not been permitted to make decisions of any significance. Her decisions, up to the time of her widowhood, probably were on the level of deciding what brand of bread to purchase. Since so many women will become widows, sexism from this perspective alone is a cruel and inhumane practice.

The educational attainment of the widow makes a significant difference in her reaction to bereavement. The less education she has, the greater will be her disorientation. This is caused by the fact that she has existed within the world without even really participating in it. She hasn't really made decisions about herself or the structure of her own world. It is difficult for her to reach out or to make new friends once her husband has died. She tends to rely on past associations and relatives, and if these do not suffice, then she gradually becomes isolated. The world had always been *his*, not *hers*. There are even women in this group who never really knew their husbands.

Conversation, outside of informational exchange, was unknown. Some have little conception of the husband's work role, outside of the fact, say, that he worked for a particular firm.

Women who belong to upper classes, on the other hand, appear to be more involved in their husband's occupational sphere. These women also have had broader educational opportunities. They were expected to appear at certain social functions, to entertain business associates, and to have enough information about the husband's area of work to converse intelligently with his associates. Such women, when the husband dies, may experience a greater sense of loss than their lower class counterparts, simply because they have more to lose in prestige, variety of roles, opportunities, and social involvement. On the other hand, however, their resources are greater, in that they probably have more money to live on and very likely can re-enter society with greater ease and develop new friendships more readily.

The most distressing aspect of widowhood for all women is the total lack of preparation for this experience. In our society, even when dying is a lingering process, death takes us unawares. The number of widows in the United States is growing. There are now more than 100,000 women widowed each year, with the average women becoming a widow at the age of fifty-six. Many of these women had never planned for a career, for single lives, or for competing roles: certainly not for widowhood.

Becoming a widow is very similar to finding one's self unexpectedly in a foreign country. Suddenly she is required to make important and costly purchases with a currency that is completely new to her, speak a language she has never before heard, and to commit herself to significant and irreversible decisions which are transmitted through an interpreter with a poor command of English. If we can appreciate the fear and bewilderment that such a situation would evoke, then we can begin to imagine what it is like to become a widow in a society that is characterized by sexism and a denial of the reality of death.

REFERENCES

Butler, R.N., & Lewis, M.I. *Aging and Mental Health.* Saint Louis: C.V. Mosby, 1977.

Caine, *Widow*. New York: W. Morrow & Co., Inc., 1974.

Cohen, K.P. *Hospice.* Germantown MD: Aspen Systems Corporation, 1979.

Kohn, J.B., & Willard, K. *THe Widower.* Boston: Beacon Press, 1978.

Lopata, H.Z. *Widowhood in an American City.* Cambridge: Schenkman, 1973.

––––––. *Women as Widows.* New York: Elsevier, 1979.

Moriarty, M., M. D., (Ed.). *The Loss of Loved Ones.* Springfield, Illinois: Charles C. Thomas, Publisher, 1967

Parkes, C. *Bereavement.* New York: International Universities Press, 1973

Resnik, H.L.P. (Ed.). *Suicidal Behaviors.* Boston: Little Brown & Co., 1968.

Schneidman, E.S. *Deaths of Man.* New York: Penguin, 1974.

Schoenberg, B. et al. *Bereavement: Its Psychosocial Aspects.* New York: Columbia University Press, 1970.

Weisman, A.D. *On Dying and Denying.* New York: Behavioral Publications, Inc., 1972.

Chapter 9

WIDOW-TO-WIDOW
The Elderly Widow and Mutual Help

*Phyllis R. Silverman
and Adele Cooperband*

Grief is often seen as an illness and programs of intervention aim at "curing" this condition. Because bereavement is a reaction that all people connected to others will experience when a loved one dies, it is essential to move away from such concepts as individual pathology and patienthood when discussing grief. Grief instead should be viewed as a psychologically appropriate and healthy reaction to a loss, and part of the human condition. One is never the same as before. People "do not work through" bereavement. Rather, in accommodating to the loss, they are changed irrevocably. The bereaved cannot be "cured" of their condition; rather, they need to learn to accept their feelings and, ultimately, to accommodate to the loss. They must learn how to build a new life without the deceased. To do this they must learn to remember the deceased while also integrating the memory of the past into the life of the present. (Silverman & Silverman, 1979).

There are really two separate issues in bereavement and widowhood that often confuse the observer as well as the individual experiencing them. The first issue is that of grief—the feelings and emotional reactions related to bereavement. Grief after the death of a loved one is expressed in crying, in restlessness, in dreams in which the deceased lives, and in feelings of pain and anguish, which are the result of the difficulty the bereaved have in understanding and accepting the loss. It does not involve guilt. Most bereaved people know remorse: they often feel *if* only, then *maybe*, but rarely do they have reason to feel conscious or unconscious guilt about the death (Parkes (1972, p. 77) has called this guilt self-reproach). Their anger with the fates that changed their lives this way does not automatically induce guilt. Unless they previously had neurotic problems that predisposed them to think in this way, or unless the circumstances were extreme, as in a suicide, they recognize that they did nothing to contribute to the death (Silverman, 1972a). The attempt to deal with guilt and anger does not help most people accommodate to the loss. If these feelings are inappropriately attributed to them the result is to make them less able to cope and more ineffectual.

The second issue, which all widowed people must meet, is related to the need to change roles. They are no longer husband or wife, but widower or widow. The social situation is different. To become a widow involves a search for a new definition of self as a single person. Without the benefit of a marital relationship which once framed and focused daily life, the widowed person must learn to live with loneliness and yet to find new purpose. It is necessary to learn to be a widow as one learns to be a wife, or mother. We are accustomed to thinking of "working at" being a wife and mother, which involves including additional people in one's life. Widowhood involves working at living without. People rarely think of becoming widowed in this way. Often the newly bereaved is expected to know immediately how to behave in this role, to have acquired this knowledge in an almost magical way. Knowledge of how to cope with grief must be made available to everyone.

Bereavement can be seen as a time of transition (Silverman et al., 1974) a process that can extend over years. During this transition the bereaved has time to accept the fact of the loss and to make the necessary accommodations psychologically and socially. An initial numbness tempers reality so that the widow is not overwhelmed by the loss. A new widow needs to learn to organize her life economically and socially to make it viable again; she needs to get perspective on her feelings, to learn what is typical for the stage she is at. She needs to learn what it means to be a widow. The role of widow is a negative one; there are few if any desirable models, so that often she is operating in a vacuum as she tries to understand what this new role status means for her and to her (Silverman, 1972b).

This paper focuses on the needs of the older widow. In many ways the elderly and the widowed suffer the same handicaps in the United States; they are alike in that no clear role redefinition is available to them, they are often socially isolated, fifth wheels, marginal to the mainstream (although from a statistical point of view this is certainly not true).

For the newly widowed, the knowledge of how to pass through this transition is not readily available. Mourning rituals and customs that formerly helped the individual accept the reality of loss and change have been cast aside. D'Enbeau (1976) in a study of attitudes toward death in a population over fifty-five concluded that the acceptance of death is learned and that such learning had not taken place among his subjects. Kastenbaum (1977) observed that in today's society people can live to advanced age before they face the loss that transforms them.

When the bereaved person cannot make this transition in an orderly manner, then maladaptive sequelae may develop. The concept of prevention is paramount, since our concern is to prevent the development of serious psychological problems in this target population. One way would be to facilitate progression through the transition for those widows who may not be able to do this for themselves. Programs to serve the bereaved would need to offer various types of help, having as their goal the amplification of the widow's coping resources to make it possible for her to accommodate and change. For many the resources required to support coping behavior can be found within their usual helping networks. For others these networks are inadequate to provide the additional information, guidance, or support needed.

• • •

THE WIDOW-TO-WIDOW PROGRAM

Silverman (1966) found that another widow is very often the most effective helper to a newly widowed person. This widow, a friend, a relative, or someone from a mutual help group provides perspective on feelings by helping the new widow understand what is typical and to be expected when she might mistake her profound and disturbing feelings as indications of an abnormal or deviant reaction. She also has a role model in the widow helper with whom she can identify.

The widow-to-widow program (Silverman, et al. 1974, 1976) was a research and demonstration project in which these ideas were tested. This model proved to be effective and today widow-to-widow programs can be found throughout the country. They are run by volunteers who are themselves widowed and who are willing to use their own experience as a resource for helping others. These volunteers reach out to the newly widowed in their own communities within a month after the death of the spouse to offer friendship and any other needed help. The widow does not have to ask for help or define herself as needy. The newly widowed do not always know what help they need. They are striving for independence, to prove to themselves that they can make it. If they need help from an agency, they are rarely sufficiently well organized to match themselves to the right one. In addition, asking for help from mental health professionals only exacerbates their feelings of being defective and their fears of being unable to manage. Help from a peer has no stigma and does not have to be defined as help. It has the quality of neighborly interest which includes the opportunity to reciprocate. The helper in this context provides a role model, friendship, some guidance, and is a bridge person facilitating the new widow's reintegration into the broader community.

The elderly (whose husbands were over sixty-five at the time of their death)[1] were not included in the original experiment. A subsequent project conducted by Adele Cooperband with Phyllis Silverman as consultant, involved a systematic outreach to a total

---

[1] Death certificates were the source of information about the death and the survivors. Only the deceased's age appears on a death certificate.

population of women including those whose husbands were all over sixty-five at the time of their deaths. This subsequent outreach with the elderly was not part of a research effort. It was sponsored by a social agency serving the Jewish community in a neighborhood in transition. The data has many limitations but we can learn something about the range of problems these widows presented, something about their reaction to an unsolicited offer of help and something about the kind of help another widow was able to offer them.

WIDOW-TO-WIDOW WITH THE ELDERLY

The program lasted for a year and a half. In this community 99 women were widowed, all over fifty years of age. It was possible to follow up on 93. Nine of the deceased husbands were between fifty and fifty-nine, 31 between sixty and sixty-nine, 39 between seventy and seventy-nine, and 14 were between eighty and eighty-nine. Two of the surviving wives were divorced or separated from their husbands for many years, and although their names appeared on the death certificates as widows, they did not consider this an accurate description of their situation. Two women moved, without leaving a forwarding address, almost immediately after the death. In addition, two of the older women died within weeks after their husbands' deaths, one letting herself die by refusing medical care, the other having been ill for some time. Subtracting these, 93 widows make up the population studied. This is not a sample. It is the total population in that community.

This is a population of primarily working-class people—lower middle class economically, but upwardly mobile in their aspirations for their children. The men earned their livings as salaried employees in a garment industry, as clerks in shops, as taxi drivers, printers, and so forth. Some were small shopkeepers. Several were very successful businessmen; one was an attorney, and one a Jewish community worker. While some women worked, they were primarily housewives, involved in homemaking and raising their children. As a group they were the workers in the local Hadassah chapter and in the synagogue sisterhood. As they grew older, they joined the Golden Age groups. They were mainly first-generation immigrants, in many ways like the group studied by Lopata (1973) in Chicago. Most had extended families in or near the community, and generally they did not concern themselves with role alternatives. They did not seek new options for themselves—when they worked it was out of necessity. Most were satisfied with role of wife, mother, and now grandmother. Being connected to their family and children was most important to them.[2]

Fifty of these widows agreed to see Mrs. Cooperband and became involved with her in some way. Twenty-two either talked to her on the telephone at length, or received her once, but while they were very friendly it was mutually agreed that they really had no need for her services. Twenty-one refused her help. Of those who refused contact, eight were unavailable. In two situations, children called and said they were caring for their mother and therefore there was no need for Mrs. Cooperband to visit; in the other six instances, the widow either did not come to the door, was never home, or did not answer the telephone. We learned about two of the latter women from neighbors: one never allowed anyone in the house, not even to offer condolences; the other was on bad terms with everyone including her children, and saw no one after she was widowed. Later, a friend got this widow involved in a women's organization where she became an officer. These responses were typical for these women and were not specific to their widowhood.

Of the other 13 who refused contact, several said they had no current need and would call if things changed later on. Several were

---

[2] Those widows most alienated from their children were, by and large, the mothers of daughters whose husbands had achieved professional status. The widow felt that the children had no time to bother with her. They, in turn, did not seem able to accept their mother's dependence on them. Trying to be understanding, she reported, "they have their own lives." However, for the most part, the surviving widow and her children seemed to accept a mutual dependence that worked well for them. Mark Zborowski in a personal communication (1970) observed that in the European Jewish traditon the elderly feel that they have earned the right to rest, to be cared for. They have no need to prove their ability to be youthful, independent, and self-sufficient. The latter attitude he observed, is an Anglo-Saxon pattern which second- and third-generation American Jews are now adopting. Most of the people in this community were immigrants who came to this country as children or young adults.

busy with their children. One woman's son had died the month before her husband. She now had a friend staying with her full-time, and she felt no need for additional assistance. She and six other of these women also worked full-time. These women did not talk at length and what they said indicated that they had family, children, and their work which kept them busy and involved. Only one woman worried the aide. She was very busy redoing her house, and this was all she talked about. The aide was concerned because she did not sound upset by the death at this time, and the quality of her preoccupation with the house seemed inappropriate. However, she appeared to be functioning adequately.

There does not seem to be any difference in age distribution between the group who were friendly but had no need of help and those who accepted help. However, differences were found when we asked whether the widows had children or relatives living nearby, were working, were well-housed, had friends, or were in good health. Those who were not in need of help had family nearby—35 percent as contrasted with 18 percent for those who accepted aid. Of the women who accepted help 68 percent lived alone, as contrasted to 56 percent who were friendly but had no need for help. Those with no need for help were more likely to be working, in good health, in more stable living situations, with adequate friendships, and having manageable reactions to their husbands' deaths.

Everyone talked about loneliness as a problem, but only those who accepted help talked of a need to meet people, make friends, and get out of the house. Important here was a need for people like themselves with whom they could socialize. The women who felt no need for help were also more likely to be taken out by their children (14 percent as compared to 8 percent) or were invited to live with them temporarily. These women were friendly, with an active network of people with whom they were involved. They saw Mrs. Cooperband in the same light, but had no reason to include her. To an extent, they were already involved in a natural or spontaneous helping network.

In a prior study of the widow-to-widow program with a similar group, a follow-up interview 3 years after the women were widowed indicated that those who did not feel the need for help had assessed their situation accurately (Silverman, 1974). This is a group identified as natural copers. However, after 3 more years, several

women in this group, in their late fifties when widowed, did begin to
have difficulties as their health failed, they lost their jobs, or were
unable to work any longer, and as the neighborhood became unsafe.
They were becoming helpless and were trapped in an oppressive
living situation. Widowhood, because they lived alone now, compounded the difficulty but did not cause it. At this point they needed
additional assistance to deal with a still different reality.

In this current population of Jewish women the characteristics
that dominate in that group who accepted the aide also indicated the
important part played by dangers in their daily life. Their husbands
had been companions and helpers, and had made them feel safer.
Before they were widowed, 30 percent of them were ill and a further 8
percent later succumbed to chronic illness, such as diabetes, heart
disease, and arthritis. Few were working. Their need for help seemed
related to the inability to maintain an active, involved life. This loss
was not necessarily due to their widowhood or only to their chronic
illness, but was more often a result of external conditions over which
they had no control, such as it being unsafe for them to go shopping.
In the first months of widowhood these women were concerned with
how to make their lives viable again. This is what they wanted Mrs.
Cooperband to help with. This is no different from what younger
widows want, to build anew a viable life.

During this period, feelings tend to come out very gradually. In
this older population the initial period of shock may be shorter.
Because of the shorthand communication between Mrs. Cooperband
and the new widow there is not a great deal of information on how
these women felt: "Adele, what can I say. You know, you are a
widow. When I get the cobwebs out of my head I want to go back to
work." In the words of another woman: "I'll be all right. I have to
get used to living without him." These women appeared to be able to
manage their bereavement and would learn to live with the
loneliness. While they did cry and were upset, they could accept the
reassurance that this was normal and that they would be all right.
They needed someone to talk to, a friendly ear, someone to complain
to. Many found this sufficient and went on to solve their own
problems. Others needed more active help. For example, some who
had the desire and means to relocate needed to be shown how to go
about moving on their own.

How the Needs of Different Widows Were Met

An example of a widow who did not require any ongoing relationship was a woman whose husband had died in his late seventies leaving a large business. She was very busy trying to settle the estate. One son was helpful, while another said that she was looking for sympathy. She was in her late sixties and had worked before her husband died. After his death, she talked about her confusion. She saw herself as usually able to manage but was now very mixed up. The son's criticism made it even more difficult. Mrs. Cooperband talked with her several times on the telephone after visiting initially. Within weeks the widow was again very busy. While not a frequent socializer and therefore not accustomed to simply visiting people, she was involved with her family and a favorite charity, which had helped her during a very difficult period in her life.

Another woman in her mid-seventies had a fleeting moment of doubt—"maybe if I had not allowed the surgery my husband might still be alive." As she talked about it she recognized that this was not so. She seemed to calm down and feel better about herself. This is a very generous, very sociable woman whom Mrs. Cooperband referred to the agency for relocation. Because she could pay full rent, the agency was able to find a place for her in a desired suburb. She spends a good deal of time with her children, one of whom is having marital difficulties, and helps with the grandchildren. This behavior is characteristic of her. She enjoys the reputation of being someone who can be counted on to help when anyone is in trouble. What she needed was an opportunity to get some perspective on her feelings. She obviously had no need to ruminate and hang on to her remorse, although she was very aware that it would not be easy to learn to live without her husband's companionship.

In contrast to the above examples were widows who needed more sustained contact. In this group one woman did feel guilty and had great need to hang on to this feeling. She had let her husband go on a trip alone because she would not leave a single sister who was very attached to her. For several years it had been the husband's regular practice to go to Florida without her. She had known that he had a heart condition, and on this last trip he had become fatally ill.

She was unable to accept any of the reassurances offered to the effect that she could not have kept him alive. In Mrs. Cooperband's words: "Her conscience was bothering her more than usual. She needed to work out her regrets. In many ways this woman was more sister than wife."

She was a chronic complainer. With Mrs. Cooperband's help, she found a real estage agent and sold her house. She moved to a new apartment and returned to work. The content of her conversation rarely changed, although her behavior did. In time she stopped calling Mrs. Cooperband. This seemed to coincide with a lessening of her need to complain. Mrs. Cooperband learned recently, through a mutual friend, that she moved to Florida with her sister, and seems to be doing well.

Mrs. Cooperband considered only one of the women "neurotic." This woman, widowed for the second time, inflicted her problem on everyone else. She felt isolated, yet could not make friends because her demanding manner put people off. This was not a new problem. She was first widowed when very young, and afterwards lived with her father, remarrying soon after his death. Her grief may have been more for her father than for her husband. She is fortunate in that her children do feel obligated to help although they rarely are able to satisfy her. Mrs. Cooperband recognized her lifelong problem and in many ways treated her like a small child being taught by its mother to make friends. In the process she did become somewhat more aware of what she did to offend people, but it is not likely that any dramatic changes occurred in her. She moved several times in search of good neighbors.

A larger group of women were offered help through the attempt to involve them with the agency and the various services it offered. Some simply needed assistance in finding subsidized housing; after Mrs. Cooperband had made the referral there was little follow-up except when the family was not served and they called to ask her to intercede. Others needed help in finding new friends; most of them did not work and might otherwise sit home alone. There was a drop-in center where people could play cards, listen to a lecture, and become involved in a variety of activities. A hot lunch was served several times a week for 50 cents. For some women it was enough to tell them about the resource for them to find their way there and become involved as they wished. One became an officer of the center's members' organization and began taking trips the group sponsored. Still others of the widows needed someone to reach out to them—to provide transportation, to help them become comfortable with the idea of joining a group. The agency for the most part was not able to do this, and in some instances Mrs. Cooperband played this role.

The value of reaching out to the widow is demonstrated by the following situation. One woman in her late seventies lived with her daughter, who was away at work all day. After her husband died, she stopped eating to the point that she lost a good deal of weight and was almost too weak to walk. Mrs. Cooperband arranged for her to be picked up once a week when a hot meal was served. She ate this because she had company, and gradually she began to feel better and to look forward to her weekly outing.

Mrs. Cooperband met a group of women who were housebound because of long-term illness. Some of them might have been able to go out if someone accompanied them. For the most part, they needed someone to drop in once a week as she did, simply to say ''hello,'' to do some shopping, sometimes to pick up their medication, or even give them a ride to the hospital in order to keep their appointment. These are neighborly acts that supplement what the family is doing, and on rare occasions provide the only support to very isolated people. In some ways Mrs. Cooperband felt these visits were most important to keep these women in contact with the larger world.

Mrs. Cooperband visited one woman who had living at home a grown retarded child whom the agency, upon the death of his father, wanted to place in an institution. Mrs. Cooperband recommended that they not do so, and supported the widow in her wish to keep the child at home. Welfare provided a homemaker several times a week to do her housework and laundry. The local priest and members of his church came in every evening to help her bathe the boy and put him to bed. Her family came to stay with the boy several times a week so that she could go out. If the boy were institutionalized, all of these links would be broken, and she would live alone in an empty house. She feared this more than anything else. While she whined and complained, she really did not want anything changed.

One woman visited had known from her sister, who had been involved in the earlier program, all about Mrs. Cooperband. This woman needed to be retrained to get a job, and the agency was able to help with this. Beyond that, she said she would be fine: her sister was helping her, as Mrs. Cooperband had helped the sister. All of this had been accomplished even though the earlier widow was a nagging, complaining woman, never satisfied with what people did for her, and her own children had given up on her. She even alienated Mrs. Cooperband. The fruits of help offered are not always immediately evident to the helper. Mrs. Cooperband's efforts were obviously successful if this widow could now be helpful to her sister. She is consciously modeling herself after Mrs. Cooperband. This is the ultlmate success of mutual help.

The purpose of talking about feelings should be to free the person to act. Offering help with feelings alone when a person does not know how to act does not in fact move the situation ahead. In helping the widowed, this is especially true, since a role lacuna often exists—and the new widow needs a role model from whom to learn how to be a widow. Often, however, for the elderly there are available role models in their peer groups. When these are working well for the widowed (given other factors in their environment) they do not need additional help. In the helping encounters described here feelings are not the primary focus. It is accepted by both parties that they exist, that it is appropriate and acceptable to express the pain, the anguish, and sorrow that are a natural part of bereavement. The widowed helper does not try to make these feelings go away. They exist, and from her accepting attitude the new widow learns to live with them and to gain perspective on them. Some widows did need a place or a relationship in which they could express their feelings, but most needed help with concrete, specific difficulties.

These difficulties were only in part related to their widowhood or age. Their reaction to being widowed was typical of all widows. In an older population bereavement is more expected, and while we presume that to a large extent the widow's reaction involves concern about her own imminent death, they did not talk about this very much. Mrs. Cooperband often felt, however, that the women over seventy-five were keeping busy with no sense of a future, waiting for death. Their role choices were more restricted, since few older women thought of building a "new life." Most often a new role involved changing patterns of interacting with people with whom they were already involved. It is almost a truism to say that the widows who had a good sense of mutuality and interpersonal competence managed this transition best. Others had more difficulty, an extension of what they were like before.

The aim of the help these widows needed appeared to be to keep them involved and connected to the world, to other people, so that they could go on living (Patterson 1974).

As the widowed elderly talk about loneliness, they grieve not only for the lost husband; what they complain about is the need for someone like themselves to talk to. While their lives may be full of people, children, grandchildren, and others, they seem to be searching for another kind of relationship—with a peer. They need someone who has reached a similar age and who can understand what they feel and what they are going through. This is the kind of sharing we typically identify with peer group relations of the teens. During critical periods in the life cycle there is a need to share experiences with others in the same situation. Young couples tend to seek each other out, and parents of young children do the same and this continues as people age as well.

As old people move away from other relationships or become more isolated (as in the move of an elderly widow to her children's home in another community), a mutual help effort can provide the opportunity for new friendships with people who have special understanding. The younger widow is isolated as well, because she is unique in her community. The need she has for a relationship with another widow may be temporary since she, in rebuilding her life, will find friends based on other needs as well. In the aged widowed the need may be permanent, since they do not have the time or resources to build a new life. It is these peer relationships that keep them in contact with life. They need someone to be like, a role model which their children cannot provide. For the first time in recorded history large numbers of people live to old age. Identifying with the young at particular critical periods in their life cycle such as the death of a spouse is not functional for an old person. They have to find in each other identities that work for this time in their life cycle. In this work mutual help groups are uniquely successful.

•   •   •

MUTUAL HELP

In this chapter we are proposing that mutual help is an alternative mode of helping that involved the positive qualities of family and community. As a fact of life, all of us participate in helping interactions, helping networks, in which we are the recipient as well as the helper. A viable life is not possible without these exchanges. These can be formalized in mutual help organizations.

Mutual help groups are defined as those organizations that limit their membership to individuals with common problems. The purpose of such organizations is to help the members and others with the same difficulties solve their mutual problems. In time, recipients of help will move to become helpers. Solutions offered usually have specific and concrete application for solving problems; help can go both ways, and is usually offered in a personal and informal fashion. Most often such groupings develop around critical transitions in a person's life, when other solutions are unavailable or ineffective. In a mutual help group, the individual is not defined as deviant or as a patient, but as someone undergoing a natural and normal experience, such as bereavement or childbirth (Silverman & Murrow, 1976).

Several conditions give rise to such organizations; they develop when the professional caregiver fails to deal successfully with the problem, when this caregiver solves a problem but does not understand or attend to the additional problems that are created by the solutions. At times of rapid social change, mutual help groups develop when there is a lacuna between existing social patterns and the requirements of new situations (Silverman, 1978-1980).

Programs for the widowed grew out of the latter situation. Social mobility, changing death rates, changing patterns of behavior and role sets in the family, as well as enormous changes in religious behavior, left a vacuum, so that patterns for grieving are not passed on by one member of the family to another. Communities are more homogeneous, so that the new widow, for example, might be unique in her community. Families move around so that their support and guidance are not readily available, nor do the patterns of previous times always seem relevant to the present situation. In a mutual help program, help can be offered spontaneously as neighbor reaches out to neighbor, thus expanding the helping network in which a person participates.

We noted earlier that in order for successful accommodation to widowhood to occur, new patterns of behavior need to be acquired. We suggest that changes in people's reactions to grief occur through an educational process. We do not see age as adversely affecting cognitive ability and learning (Monge & Gardner, 1972). Tough (1977) has discussed the remarkable amount of adult learning that goes on each year. Over 70 percent of this learning is either self-planned or dependent on the adult's friends and peer group. Tough has described a learning project as a highly deliberate effort to gain and retain certain definite knowledge and skill or to change in some other way. The person has a task (e.g., raising a child) and learns certain knowledge and skills in order to perform the task successfully.

What facilitates learning in a mutual help group? Schachtel (1959), reporting on a study of affiliative tendencies in college students during periods of anxiety, observes that subjects chose to be alone under stress rather than with people who had not shared their experience. He concludes that:

> ...under conditions of anxiety the affiliative tendency is highly directional.... Whatever the needs aroused by the manipulation of anxiety, it would seem that their *satisfaction demands the presence of others in a similar situation.*

Schachtel's findings help to explain the appeal of mutual help groups to people in times of stress. There is a need to find someone like themselves so that they no longer feel alone or unique. Schachtel suggests that it is easier to learn in a setting with people who are having the same experience. In every mutual help group with which we talked, members expressed the relief they felt in finally being able to share what they were feeling with someone else "like me."

Bandura (1977) has described three approaches to learning: modeling, vicarious learning (seeing others perform threatening activities without adverse consequences), and verbal persuasion. He notes that people can be persuaded that they possess the capability to master a difficult situation, but, unless they are provided with effective aids for action, they are unlikely to learn. Modeling provides the opportunity to learn, from other people's experience, that changes are possible and subsequently to learn how to make similar changes.

Bandura (1977) observed that people may develop models for themselves from their own experience. However, people in transition often do not have this experience. He suggests that with role models and effective aids, learning and change take place for people who have no prior experience coping with the situation in which they now find themselves. Mutual help experiences provide the opportunity to find a role model in "someone like me" and to learn vicariously what is needed to make necessary changes. Mutual help groups can be successful where others, such as members of the formal human service system cannot because these conditions are inherently present.

CONCLUSION

The quality of life in a family and the spirit of cooperation in a neighborhood may determine how an individual participates in any helping network. Formal mutual help organizations may serve to develop and stimulate reciprocal networks where the individual will expand his repertoire of coping techniques. In the life cycle there are many natural helping networks. People play various roles in them; in the role of parent and child the child is mainly a recipient of care. In the roles of husband and wife there is more mutuality The elderly have much to give. Who are the natural recipients of their helping impulses? They have a lifetime of experience. Who will learn from them? They also need to be cared for. There must be a way here of nurturing mutuality and reciprocal giving and receiving of care. In the long run, we are talking about preparing people for the normal role changes that will take place in their lives, changes in the helping roles they will play and in their roles as recipients of help as well.

The basic dignity of humankind is expressed in our capacity to be involved in reciprocal helping relationships. Out of this compassion comes cooperation; only then is it possible to build a community. The quality of life of any individual is affected by the nature and quality of the helping networks or exchanges in which the person participates. By facilitating and enhancing these networks, it may be possible to prevent or alleviate psychological stress and improve the quality of life in any community.

REFERENCES

Bandura, A. *Social Learning Theory*. Englewood Cliffs, New Jersey: Prentice Hall, 1977.

D'Enbeau, M.S. The Process of Coming to Terms with Death as a Psychic Energy Release. Unpublished Ph.D. dissertation. Dissertation Abstracts International, 1976.

Kastenbaum, R. Death and Development Through the Lifespan. In Feifel, H. (Ed.) *New Meaning of Death*. New York: McGraw Hill, 1977.

Lopata, H. *Widowhood in an American City*. Cambridge, Mass.: Schenkman Publishing Co., 1973.

Monge, R., & Gardner, E.F. *A Program of Research in Adult Differences in Cognitive Performance and Learning: Backgrounds for Adult Education and Vocational Retraining*. Final Report. Washington, D.C.: Office of Education (DHEW), January 1972.

Parkes, C.M. *Bereavement: Studies of Grief in Adult Life*. New York: International Universities Press, 1972.

Patterson, R.D., Abrahams, R., & Baker, F. Preventing Self Destructive Behavior. *Geriatrics,* 1974.

Schachtel, S. *The Psychology of Affiliation,* Stanford; Stanford University Press, 1959.

Silverman, P.R. Anticipatory Grief from Perspective of Widowhood. In B. Schoenberg, et al. (Eds.) *Anticipatory Grief.* New York: Columbia University Press, 1974.

———. MacKenzie, D., Pettipas, M., & Wilson, E., Eds. *Helping Each Other in Widowhood.* New York; Health Services Publishing Corp., 1974, pp. 101-105.

———. *If You Will Lift the Load, I Will Lift It Too.* New York: *Jewish Funeral Directors of America,* 1976.·

———. Intervention With the Widow of a Suicide. In A.C. Cain, (Ed.) *Survivors of Suicide,* Springfield, Ill.; Charles C. Thomas, 1972a, pp. 186-214.

_____ & Murrow, H. Mutual Help During Critical Role Transitions. *The Journal of Applied Behavioral Science,* 1976, *12*(3): 410-418.

_____. *Mutual Help Groups and the Role of the Mental Health Professional.* Washington, D.C.: U.S. Governmental Printing Office, NIMH, DHEW Publication No. (ADM) 78-646. Spring 1978.

_____. *Mutual Help Groups: Organization and Development,* Beverly Hills, Ca.: Sage Publishing Co., 1980.

_____. Services for the Widowed During the Period of Bereavement. In *Social Work Practice.* New York: Columbia University Press, 1966, pp 170–189.

_____. The Widow As a Caregiver in a Program of Preventive Intervention with Other Widows. *Mental Hygiene,* 1970, *54,* 540-547.

_____. The Widow-to-Widow Program: An Experiment in Preventive Intervention. *Mental Hygiene,* 1969, *53,* 333-337.

_____. Widowhood and Preventive Intervention. *The Family Coordinator,* 1972b, *21,* 95-102.

Tough, A. *Major Learning Efforts: Recent Research and Future Directions.* Adult Education, xxviii, *4,* Summer 1978.

Chapter 10

NOW, FOR THE FEMINIST MENOPAUSE THAT REFRESHES! Or: Creative Leadership of Older Women

Wilma Scott Heide*

DEAR SISTERS AND BROTHERS:

This chapter will be a letter to readers, a rather lengthy one. I'm comfortable with a letter; it seems more personalized, or at least less depersonalized than an essay. I trust you'll be comfortable with this approach, as well as with my title, "NOW, For the Feminist Menopause That Refreshes." I've also chosen that for deliberate reasons which I want to share.

Much writing about women in general, and older women in particular, focuses on older women as people "acted upon," as victims, as people with problems, or affected by others. All of this has the ring of considerable reality. However, these phenomena are not

*Former Chairone of Board, then President of NOW, National Organization for Women, Inc.

the total reality, so I want to focus on some other dimensions. These include older women as actors,* as leaders, as healers, as creators, as visionaries. Many older women are unsung *she*roes (heroine is a derivative word and thus inappropriate) of our time and of all times. I will sing of these remarkable women either in the text of this letter, or at its end. Many of them make things happen, as well as have things happen to them.

I will also share some concepts, premises, and my value perspectives. Much of this will mean some reconceptualizing of fairly commonly held beliefs and ideas. This will include demythologizing those "old husbands' tales," some of which are believed by some women and not necessarily by all men. For example: there's a myth in this nation that women control the wealth in the U.S.A. and much of the rest of the world. The facts are that women actually control only 17 percent of the wealth (in terms of economic resources) in the U.S.A.[1] For a woman to have money in her name (nominal wealth) does not necessarily mean she controls it or administers it, or even owns it. More often than may be generally known, this wealth is actually controlled by husbands and/or other men, by male-run economic institutions, in some states by laws granting control of women's resources or shared property to husbands and fathers, or other men. Money actually controlled by men is often in a woman's or girl's name as a tax dodge for men. So, women's "control" of U.S. wealth is much more apparent than real.

A myth related to the woman "controlling most of the wealth" fiction is that about widows and divorced women being wealthy. There are some wealthy women who are widowed or divorced. Their affluence is noted in various communication media on a dramatic scale that distorts the reality of most women's real lives.

"Statistics show that the majority of older women (of the U.S.A.), live in poverty or near-poverty. In the late 1970s, only 5 percent of single women over sixty-five had annual income in excess

*Actress, waitress, hostess, stewardess, are derivative words for people who are not derivative of, and secondary to men, all Adam's Rib mythology being precisely that. Women and men are actors, waiters, hosts, and stewards.

of $5,000, and the trend is toward an increasing number in this situation.''[2]

So much for the mythology of women "controlling" most of U.S. wealth. Worldwide, the truth of women's real economic wealth is even bleaker. From the International Labor Organizaton, a part of the United Nations, we learn the following: worldwide, women do 66 percent of the world's work of all kinds (in and out of the home); women hold 33 percent of the *paid* jobs in the world; women receive 10 percent of the money paid for work (out of all that is paid for work—yet, women do 66 percent of the work); women own *at most* 1 percent of the world's property.[3] I trust you note that I'm *not* writing that women *earn* given percentages in relation to what men *earn*; I'm writing that women are *paid* the stated amounts, though women may actually *earn* much more.

Some other fiction to demythologize includes the imagery that women marry houses. No so, though the term "housewife" surely suggests it. Homemaker is a more accurate word that can convey the reality that homemaking is for all those of *both* sexes who live in a home. The concept, head of household, is becoming an anachronism, thanks to feminists. It was always problematic. It was used to denote the real or presumed economic providers. Being the economic providers should not be assumed to give' that or those provider(s) political or legal prerogatives as suggested by the phrase "head of household." Economic provider, besides being more accurate, delineates, and more precisely describes, what is provided and implicitly acknowledges that other valuable contributions are necessary for social units of all kinds of families. Thus, the social, labor, psychological, emotional, reproductive, and maintenance contributions to an ongoing social unit can be, and are becoming valued, as well as economic contributions. Why, therefore, except consequent to patriarchy, even assume that there needs to be a "head of household," and/or that being the only economic provider (or simply being male) entitles one to headship status?

In 1965, I wrote a 12-part series for a coalition of newspapers in Pennsylvania. The series was called *Poverty is Expensive*[4] because that is the most significant reality of poverty, i.e., it costs more to be poor. What an irony, what a paradox! The poorest in our land are women of all races, and our dependent children. Older women are the demographically largest segment of the poor in the U.S.A. In all adult age groups, women of color, disproportionate to their percentage of the population, experience the most acute economic poverty. The most hopeful sign for women of all ages and races and ethnic populations is the organizing as, and/or with, feminists for significant action.

Ronnie Reagan and his white male club and supporters are unwittingly serving as great recruiters for change agents, galvanized into action by insensitive policies, practices, and budget cutting most damaging to those already poor. Ronnie always had trouble getting good parts and good scripts; now, he has a good part, but a lousy script and uncaring, militaristic (redundant?) script writers.

To continue the demythologizing: older women activists and other feminists know the issues are not women versus men, black versus white, the older versus the younger, or any other androcentric, adversarial dichotomies. The issues, I think, represent value transformations from past to present to future visions and realities, from dominance by affluent, white, heterosexist male values to multicultural feminist values. Since feminism, among other things, affirms the "feminine" qualities as the more humane in *both* sexes for private and public policies, it portends the transcendence of either/or, adversarial (versus), pro/con, dominance/submission kinds of thinking and societies. In these and related ways, feminists are futurists, who are integrating the personal and political, the private and public, and the more life-affirming potentials of both the "feminine" and "masculine" qualities of both sexes.

It is not true, as Betty Friedan wrote,[5] that feminists did not see the possible trap of no-fault divorce in the absence of a prerequisite of built-in economic security for the previously economically dependent spouse as part of the terms of the divorce. Most feminists did see the trap and acted to prevent no-fault divorce legislation without prior economic securities. It is true that Friedan did not see the trap until later. Neither she nor any other individual or organization, as she again implies in her most recent book,[6] *is* the women's movement. She and others need to be careful not to equate economic dependence with dependence per se; the two are not necessarily concomitant. Virtually all women work; *some* are paid.

Part of feminism's life-affirming values and reconceptualizing of functions is the thought that homemakers need social security in their own right, and veteran's benefits. Homemaking that includes pregnancy and childbirth is life-risking, child and spouse care is life-affirming; all this plus home care is national, as well as personal service. Homemakers are veterans and surely in less destructive and lethal ways than much of military service. Also, homemakers are influenced by implicit and explicit national policies, a justification for benefits to military veterans. Besides, homemakers are the largest occupational class in society.

To continue both the demythologizing and reconceptualizing, I want to address so-called "humor" that is misogynist. An example is "jokes" about mothers-in-law. These are cruel and insensitive gibes at women who devote their lives to their children (as society has prescribed or dictated) and who may have difficulty breaking two decades of habit, only to be insulted for continuing to "live" through others. I advocate that any woman or man who cares about women stop these would-be comedians publicly or privately by speaking up and saying, "You insult all women, which is not funny."

Indeed, one way to create our own terms for humor is to do a take-off on some of the sexist and agist double standards, including those perpetuated in advertising. It would seem that women get wrinkles and men get wiser with the years. A friend, Judy Pickering and I, conducted a humor workshop at a NOW Eastern Regional Conference several years ago. As part of that program, we created a (hypothetical) cream which we'll call "Youth Away"* for women. We made aging, including wrinkles, a plus, and advertised "Youth Away" to hasten the time when one could be rid of that unsightly smooth characterless skin.

Other approaches represent examples of how people may decide our own terms to approach and create phenomena. The phrase "Black is beautiful!" was a stroke of genius; it turned what was considered by some to be negative (black) into a positive concept and image. One of the too unsung sheroes of feminism and now President of the Older Women's League, OWL, is Tish Sommers. In 1973, I asked her to initiate a committee in NOW** to organize with older women for action. I also asked her and the committee to look into the situations of homemaking women displaced by desertion, death

* Creation of Mary Klindt of Sangamon State University.

**NOW, National Organization for Women, Inc.

and/or divorce. Out of that, Tish and many other sisters developed the name and concept Displaced Homemakers, generated legislation, and founded programs to address their needs.

The displacement of homemakers (mostly women) was not new; what was new was creative and organized attention to their needs by themselves and others. To learn about the process of development of the Displaced Homemaker Movement, read the book by one of the women who, with Tish Sommers, provided significant leadership, Laurie Shields,[7] another unsung shero, along with Maggie Kuhn of the Gray Panthers and NOW, Marjorie Collins, editor of *Prime Time* and NOW member.

One of the first things Tish did in organizing the NOW Older Women's Committee was to issue a press release invitation to her imminent ''Fine 59th Birthday'' as a recruitment get-together. The graphics on the Birthday invitation included a woman on a broomstick saying ''Me retire? I've just begun to fly!'' This, and other creative organizing actions represent ways that Tish, Maggie, Marjorie, and Laurie, and thousands of others put the situations of older people, most of whom are women, on the national agenda and are influencing, if not determining, public policy and practice. Representataive Claude Pepper of Florida is already publicly recognized as an effective advocate for older Americans.

For over 10 years, many of us, as feminists, had noted how the Social Security laws, practices, and administration actively discriminated against women in countless ways. Finally, in 1979, the documentation of these assertations was presented in an extensive report.[8] This report might never have been produced without pressure from the feminist movement in general, and the Older Women's movement in particular. Older folks have friends in Congress, including some older people who are pushing legislation to implement multiple recommendations of that report. These include the need for a homemaker to have social security in his/her own right, not as an appendage to the breadwinner.

We've all heard that the social security system is in financial trouble. The Reagan people tell us the only two ways to 'solve' the problems are either to increase payroll taxes or cut benefits. That's the old androcentric either/or approach, and is bound further to hurt those already hurting. Feminists transcend either/or problem identification and problem solving. For instance, the Older Women's

League recommends some "painless alternatives to the social security problem"[9] involving neither benefit cuts nor payroll tax increases. OWL's approach is both for the short term and long term. This includes: using part of the (oil) windfall profits tax (for short term infusion), value added tax (V.A.T.), taking social security out of the unified budget, changes in Trust Fund accounting, a merger of different social security funds, interfund borrowing, extending social security coverage to uncovered workers, augmenting the trust funds from other sources (demographic changes modify both needs and resources), improving investment policies of Social Security Trustees, making benefit changes that would aid the poorest (mostly women), and ending subsidies to the more affluent (mostly men) who don't need it.

In the foregoing reconceptualizing and in what follows, older women activists are not denying the realities of aging and problems that often accompany this process, but are also affirming the liberaton to be and to become. In part, it's the old optimist/pessimist observation transcended, i.e., is one-half a glass of water half full or half empty; and how about transcending this by "Turning on the tap,"[10] to fill the glass, and one's life?

Next, I want to list and reference actions advocated by others and/or myself. The fuller development of these, and other ideas, would require at least a book, and many are already in motion by the Older Women's League, O.W.L. members and friends, and some members of the Gray Panthers.

1. Older women need to 'study' older women and determine the public policies that affect our lives. This suggests significant changes in what is researched and who does the research and for what purposes. Gerontologists include few women; often talk to each other *about* older women; may hold academic credentials but be experientially sexist, racist, agist, classist, and homophobic. No wonder Irene Pauli writes "Gerontologist—Ho Hum. It's a good thing we don't dig their jargon, or we'd get mad."[11] Action advocated: insist that we 'study' ourselves and from feminist perspectives; insist that public money go to recipients geared for action research, not obscure studies that collect dust, but make no qualitative difference in our lives.

2. Older women need to be the majority of staff for any programs addressed to our needs. Across the country, this is currently not true.[12] As Carole Runions of OWL advocates, just as mothers and daughters are becoming more mutually supportive, so must older and younger women, in general, communicate and share our talents and live experiences that transcend our age differences.

3. Support and advocate the move* to require that no public body, commission, board, or cabinet at any level have a majority of more than one of either sex and that such bodies be demographically representative as well by race, age, income level.[13]

4. Visit legislators and public officials; it will do great things for your self-confidence; indeed, as have many others, you may decide to become and *be* legislators and public officials.

5. Be court and agency watchers and monitors to assure that what legislation and regulations we have to prohibit agism, as well as sexism and racism, are complied with. A rather new term for those advocating for the older Americans, is Geriadvocacy.

6. Insist that research done on the elderly separate the data on older women and older men, whose circumstances are not identical. Because this is seldom done, most people don't realize that most older women are poor, but most older men are not. The same breaking down of data is needed vis a vis older people of color and older white people, wherein the former are more economically impoverished.

7. Monitor pension and benefit plans. We're just beginning to get some sex-neutral policies and practices. Prior to 1972, even the Equal Employemnt Opportunities Commission (EEOC) charged with enforcement of Title VII of the 1964 Civil Rights Law, and the 1972 Equal Employment Opportunity Law accepted employers' and insurance companies' sexist policies and practices. This meant EEOC accepted that since women, on the average, live 7 years longer than men, women should receive less benefits, though they paid in the same amount, or, to receive the same benefits should pay in more than men.

* From an idea first initiated by Jo Ann Evans Gardner in Allegheny County, Pennsylvania.

In 1972, a group of us from NOW met with EEOC commissioners to effect change in EEOC views and policies. I reminded the commissioners that it is also true that, on the average, white people live 7 years longer than black people. To be consistent with their policies vis a vis the sexes, EEOC should therefore insist either that white people pay more than black people, to receive the same benefits or that white people should pay in the same as black people, but receive less benefits. The commissioners agreed they were inconsistent, yet were not about to change policies. Only my promise (not threat) of a legal mandamus action and a press conference the next day to expose their sexism persuaded them to change their policies to a sex-neutral posture and practice, as the laws they were charged to enforce mandated they do consistently.[14]

8. The Equal Right Amendment (ERA) to the U.S. Constitution states: "Equality of rights under the law shall not be denied or abridged by the United States or any of the States on account of sex." The States (35) having 72 percent of U.S. population have ratified it. Sixty-two percent of the (15) unratified states populations support it. As of this writing (3/82), 3 more states are needed to ratify it by 6/30/82. Here are actions I advocate: if and when the ERA is ratified, monitor federal, state, and local laws and government to see that it is implemented (states have 2 years to comply); if, in spite of the clear majority support, 3 of the remaining states fail to ratify by the current deadline, support the move to begin all over again on July 1, 1982 to assure U.S. constitutional equality of the sexes by law.

In addition, remembering the majority support (62 percent) of E.R.A. which rises to 80 percent when people know what E.R.A. *actually* states (not just what they think it states), some additional actions of time and U.S.A.-honored nature are indicated if state legislatures fail us by 6/30/82. This nation was founded on the principle that taxation without representation is tyranny; equally true is the principle that taxation with *mis*representation is tyranny. Therefore, given the overwhelming majority (62 to 80 percent) support for ERA, women and supportive men should pay no taxes until constitutional equality of women and men is a reality. There are

risks; this *is* a civil disobedience. There are continuing risks if
we continue to support laws and governments that allow second
class citizenship for the majority of its people—women and
girls. Older women are among those who most need ERA.

9. Next, be informed about, support, and advocate the feminist
health movement in the U.S.A., and throughout the world. We
are demystifying the M. Diety; desexigrating health care
occupations and professions. Indeed, deprofessionalizing is an
issue, as part of demystification and the valuation of self-
knowledge and self-care. We are creating feminist alternatives
to the medical (disease-oriented and patriarchal) model of so-
called health care.[15] We are moving away from the
superordinate-subordinate physician-nurse interrelationship in
law and in practice, to a complementary, more holistic model of
health care. In that model, medicine is part of and/or may
augment other health care, but does not control it.

It is pathological for a disease and instrumentally-oriented
field (medicine) to dominate that holistic health care, which
does or can go far beyond mere medical care. This is not to say
that physicians are good for nothing, but that they are not good
for everything. Feminist values and principles are integral to
health care that is holistic. Nor am I advocating that nurses
practice medicine without a license; but I am advocating that
physicians stop trying to practice nursing without a nursing
license.[16] One of many examples of a new feminist health
literature is the writing of Barbara Seaman and her husband,
Gideon,[17] who may save your life with documented knowledge
about what is and is not good for you. Older women, especially,
though not only, need to know the truth abut estrogen, for
instance.

10. Consider women's studies as basic, required education for all
health care providers and anyone else who works with and
influences human beings. At my own current place of
institutional affiliation, Sangamon State University in Illinois,
we in women's studies consider the study of women, as subject,
not objects, as central to the study of all humankind and all
human affairs, just as we consider the study of people of color.
The phenomenon of essentially white male studies, albeit with

other names, perpetuates the utter social illiteracy about women of all races and men of color. This is one of many reasons that the situations and talents of older women are nearly invisible even, if not especially, to those who are "educated."

11. In higher education, one of the phenomena of the past decade is the great number of women, especially middle-aged and older, flocking to campuses throughout the U.S.A. Some of these are called re-entry women for whom there are still barriers, financial and other, in androcentric (male-centered) institutions. The Project on the Status and Education of Women ably led by Bernice Resnick Sandler has four excellent Field Evaluation Drafts on Re-entry Women that delineate both problems and solutions.[18] The education you start or restart and validate may be your own; education does mean the act of leading forth. It implies change; we therefore trust the educators are educable about women and everyone else.

One good campus organizing focus and issue is the phenomenon of credit for prior learning, CPL. This has profound implications, not only but especially for older women who often have learned (and can teach) much that may be undervalued and for which we have seldom received any credit (except on Mother's Day), as attested by Sangamon State University's institutional change agent, Phyllis Walden.

12. In essence, what I'm advocating is that, while agonizing and honest expressions of justified anger are healthy, they are not enough. Move from agonizing to organizing for action that makes a difference. The action itself is a healthy and educational process. If you want to learn something, try to teach it; if you really want to understand something, work to change it. It could be a credo for political activists. OWL has an organizing manual that will send your spirits soaring.[19]

At the beginning of this open letter, I promised to sing about some unsung sheroes and I have, but I want to mention some additional sheroes who have influenced me and millions of others; poet, writer, actor Maya Angelou (who also uses the word shero, instead of heroine), Eleanor Roosevelt whom I met in 1945, Dorothy Height with whom I've worked, Jessie Bernard, dear friend and brilliant sociologist/feminist and finally, my own favorite Mother, Ada Long Scott. She's no feminist but I admire her periodic acts of courage in spite of a male-dominated socialization and culture. She has some trouble identifying with much of what I'm about, just as I, as a child, was radicalized to becoming a feminist, partly because I could not identify with her being so male-identified and so denying of her own worth. She does understand when I affirm that feminism portends the power of love (in the sense of caring about ourselves and others), exceeding the love of power. So, sisters and brothers, do I hope that you understand.

Sincerely,

Wilma Scott Heide

REFERENCES

1. NOW Stockholder Action/Policy Studies, 1973, NOW Action Center, 425 13th Street N.W., Washington, D.C. 20004.

2. MacLean, J. (Ed.). *Growing Numbers, Growing Force, A Report from the White House Mini-Conference on Older Women, October 11-12,* 1980. Published by Older Women's League Educational Fund, 3800 Harrison Street, Oakland, California 94611, and Western Gerontology Society, 785 Mark Street, Suite 1114, San Francisco, California 94103, p. 43.

3. United Nations Commission on the Status of Women, Report #3 in preparation for the Mid-Decade (of the International Women's Decade 1975-85) Conference in Copenhagen, Denmark, from the International Labor Organization, 1980.

4. Heide, W.S. *Poverty is Expensive.* c/o New Kensington Dispatch, New Kensington, PA 15068, Summer 1965.

5. Friedan, B. *It Changed My Life.* New York: Random House, 1976, pp. 325-26.

6. Heide, W.S. A Critique of Friedan's 'Critique' of Feminism. *Spokeswoman,* National Feminist News Monthly, 906 National Press Building, Washington, D.C. 20045, Vol. XI, No. 11, November 1982, p. 1.

7. Shields, L. *Displaced Homemakers,* Organizing For a New Life with Epilogue by Tish Sommers. New York: McGraw Hill, 1981.
8. Social Security Administration, U.S. Dept. of Health and Human Services. *Social Security and the Changing Roles of Men and Women.* Washington, D.C., February 1979.
9. Older Women's League, OWL, *Painless Alternatives to the Social Security Problem.* 3800 Harrison Street, Oakland, California 94611, Sept. 23, 1981. $1.00 for print and mailing costs (my idea.)
10. McLean, J. (Ed.). op. cit. *Growing Numbers, Growing Force,* p. 20.
11. Pauli, I. Commentary in *Everybody's Studying Us,* The Ironies of Aging in the Pepsi Generation; with cartoons by Bulbul, Glide Publications, 330 Ellis St., San Francisco, CA 94102, 1976, p. 51.
12. MacLean, J. (Ed.). *Growing Numbers, Growing Force,* op. cit. p. 16.
13. Crater, F. *The Woman Activist,* Inc., 2310 Barbour Road, Falls Church, Virginia 22043.
14. From author's notes on meeting and EEOC Statement of Proposed Regulations in Federal Register, later adopted.
15. Ruzek, S.B. *The Women's Health Movement,* Feminist Alternatives to Medical Control. Praeger, New York: 1978.
16. Heide, W.S. Feminism Making a Difference in Our Health. In M.T. Notman & C.C. Nadelson (Eds.), *The Woman Patient* (Vol. 1). New York: Plenum Publishing Corp., [DATE], pp. 9–20.
17. Seaman, B. & Seaman, G. *Women and the Crisis in Sex Hormones.* New York: Rawson Association Publishers, Inc., 1977.
18. Project on the Status and Education of Women, Association of American Colleges, 1818 R. Street N.W., Washington, D.C. 20009.
19. OWL, Organizing Manual, 3800 Harrison Street, Oakland, California 94611. $4.00, Loose-leaf and in continual process.

BIBLIOGRAPHY FOR CREDIT FOR PRIOR LEARNING, CPL, FOLLOW-UP:

1. American National Red Cross, "I Can, Adviser's Manual," Collaboration for Volunteer Development, 1981.
2. Forrest, Aubrey, *Assessing Prior Learning,* a CAEL (Cooperative Assessment of Experiential Learning) Student Guide, American City Building, Suite 403, Columbia, Indiana 21044.

Chapter 11

POLICY DIRECTIONS AND PROGRAM DESIGN
Issues and Implications in Services for Older Women

Marcia B. Steinhauer
and Stefanie S. Auslander

INTRODUCTION

Many times you are aware of the older woman in your life. She may be an aging mother, a favorite aunt, or a neighbor who always had a fresh batch of cookies to offer. Other times, the other aging woman around you is not even noticed. She is there and yet faceless to all. She sits in department stores by the elevators and watches the crowds. Downtown cafeterias and lunch counters are habitual haunts. She might carry large paper bags crammed with valued mementos as she continues to be part of the walking scene. Hats long out of fashion and rouged circles for cheeks are the outward efforts at appearing feminine and young.

It is these women and their unique problems that are of increasing importance as a policy focus. The tasks and responsibilities of policy makers and program designers are threefold: to enhance public awareness of older women; to stimulate and conduct research and disseminate findings; and to develop support services and community resources designed to benefit older women. The intent of this chapter is to delineate for those in policy-making positions some of the issues in designing services for older women.

. This chapter reviews the major characteristics of older females as a background for a discussion of program issues. Against this background, three subject areas are highlighted: target population identification; initial services; and appropriate providers.

DESCRIPTIVE DIMENSIONS OF THE OLDER WOMAN

If policy makers are to address the problems of the female segment of the aging population, then an appreciation of the major characteristics is basic. While each older woman is indeed unique as an individual, there are several especially noteworthy dimensions that can lend to the construction of a group portrait. The double jeopardy and stigmatism of agism and sexism are the outstanding characteristics. Older females belong to two social minority groups that face both discrimination and lack of power. The discrimination might be either deliberate and unmistakable or of a benign-neglect variety. The combination of agism and sexism toward older women is witnessed by negative media images, newly relegated poverty status, and sparse employment opportunities.

A second descriptive characteristic of older women is the multiple role changes occurring for them in mid and later years. The changing marital status into widowhood, returning to school, ending active parenting, relating to children as adults, and coping with aging parents are but a few role areas that can bring stress and lower morale. Suddenly being a different person with no preparation for unfamiliar expectations can be a jarring experience.

The health status of older females is a particularly complex dimension that is important to policy makers. Some highlights of physical and mental health problems are illustrative. Osteoporosis, or "thinning of the bone," is the most serious ailment of postmenopausal females. Because of reduced calcium intake, females are more prone to loss of bone integrity and consequent loss of mobility. Thus approximately 90 percent of all hip fractures occur in postmenopausal women suffering from osteoporosis.

Another cause of physical and emotional illness in older women is the higher incidence of breast and uterine cancer during postmenopausal years. While many women could, ordinarily, take hormone treatments to help stabilize physically induced depression caused by hormone imbalances, those women who have had cancer of the female organs are often urged to reduce estrogen intake. Not only do these women suffer from the normal depression associated with major surgery, often mutilating, but they must also cope with possible depression because of an uncertain future in terms of cancer reoccurrence. Furthermore, the use of nonhormonal drugs to alleviate depression may sometimes trigger abuse patterns.

Also among the serious problems affecting elderly women are vulvar and vaginal changes that may predispose women to infection and bleeding during sexual intercourse. Urinary tract infections and stress incontinence are common sources of discomfort and embarrassment. Visual impairment, hypertension, arthritis, diabetes, and senile dementia are also more common among older women. Additionally, the cosmetic aspects of aging skin are of importance to this group.

Another health problem of the female aged is that of the low morale and depression associated with wives of elderly disabled men. These women, themselves, may suffer from chronic ailments associated with aging; but their problems are compounded because they must also care for husbands whose problems may be more debilitating than their own. The burden of care is consequently placed on one whose own health may be failing. This can cause serious morale or emotional problems.

Because women live longer, the physical and emotional problems associated with elderly women are indeed factors which must be addressed if the quality of their extended life is to be good. Services and programs can be designed to have positive impacts on the health of older females. For example, nutrition programs which emphasize increased calcium intake for older women can be instrumental in the prevention of hip fractures. Similarly, increased home care services to assist women caring for disabled husbands could improve their overall emotional status.

The combination of the absence of role change preparation and a changing physical condition promote the fourth descriptive dimension that should be of interest to policy makers. While all elderly fear being victims of crime, females appear to be especially fearful of victimization. The crimes cover a spectrum from fraudulent schemes in home repair and insurance policies to the physically violent one of rape and abuse. Unfamiliarity with financial management and an increasingly restricted ability to defend their persons put older women into a variety of potentially dangerous situations.

The concluding descriptive dimension of the group portrait of older women is their reluctance to assert themselves in maintaining or bettering their circumstances. Lifelong patterns of taking whatever was dealt them or deferring to dominant male counterparts is not a preparatory mindset for assertive behavior. Older women accept their fate and try to be content. This ingrained reluctance or inability to make their needs known is an existing and real problem for program designers. This reluctance is a serious obstacle to accessing existing or created services.

The lack of homogenity in this group is evidenced by a broad differentiation in characteristics. However, this selection of descriptive dimensions of the female elderly serves as a background for the subsequent exploration of program issues. Those to be discussed in the next sections are an outgrowth of this group portrait of older women. Their unique problems demand clarification and special attention toward resolution.

ISSUES IN SERVICES AND PROGRAMS

The older woman as a focus for program development is a newly discovered concern. Awareness of problems has already beem witnessed in the literature and at professional conferences, but interest in translating problems into solution activities is recent. Attention to program issues for women is in addition to the traditional service delivery planning and structural considerations of: age-segregated vs. generic services; centralized vs. decentralized organizations; or direct provisions vs. purchase of service arrangements. Thus, the concerns of how to organize the delivery of services to older females are not as salient in this discussion as are the actual programs to be designed. The major issues for policy determination centered on older women which will be addressed in this segment are: target population identification; initial services; and appropriate providers.

Target Population Identification

One of the primary obstacles to program delivery to older women is identifying them as a target population. Locating them in the community as people with needs can be difficult. The casual observer cannot tell when some people are in need. Many, while owning homes and appearing well-dressed, are rapidly depleting meager savings. Beyond casual observational techniques, there is no formal mechanism for identifying and targeting services directly to older women. The formal needs-assessment mechanisms do not recognize and establish women as a distinct group. Elderly target groups, as addressed in the Older Americans Act, are usually defined in terms of extreme age, ethnic background, or income level. Individuals seventy-five years and over, of minority status, isolated, or with poverty characteristics are all recognized as designated group members with official and appropriate service priorities. From a policy and resource perspective, women are considered a part of "all elderly" and thus their needs have not been established and recognized as being distinct for resource allocation purposes. The obvious implication of this issue is to modify the formal needs-assessment mechanisms to identify older females as a specific priority group. A subsequent implication is to direct monetary resources to services for this defined subpopulation.

Initial Services

To meet the pervasive situations and needs of existing in a lengthening life cycle, a great range and variety of services and programs are required. The impossibility of addressing all service needs is evident. Therefore, the second major issue for exploration is the selection of possible services for initial emphasis and implementation. The selection of proposed programs is intended to be congruent with the philosophy of elderly remaining in the community at their highest level of independence. The suggested initial emphasis for female-oriented programs includes the areas of health, education, outreach, income maintenance and respite care.

•   •   •

HEALTH CARE SERVICES

The range of health problems of the older woman as previously discussed, can be addressed by three health service orientations, including acute, chronic, and preventive approaches. Acute care services are those provided for illnesses or problems requiring immediate attention. Bronchial attacks, flu, broken hips, intestinal tract viruses, and pneumonia are all examples of conditions needing immediate care. Chronic disorders include both physical and emotional problems which require long-term care and/or are debilitating to some degree. Preventive health care includes those services aimed at early detection of disease.

Acute and chronic health care services can be provided by a wide range of medical personnel and in a variety of settings. Hospitals, clinics, private physicians' offices, and health departments are among these settings. Physicians, nurses, pharmacists, and other allied health personnel are the providers. The problem for the elderly is twofold. They must have access to acute health care services and they must understand when the receipt of these services is necessary.

Preventive services may reduce the incidence of chronic conditions. One of the more serious chronic health problems is malnutrition. The two varieties of malnutrition can also complicate other health problems. Overnutrition, or obesity, is a problem the general population experiences, but which becomes more dangerous with increasing age. Undernutrition, or lack of proper nourishment, is often a manifestation of the social isolation and low income of elderly persons. Thus, nutrition services such as meals-on-wheels or congregate eating programs are an important aspect of treatment for the chronically ill. Nutrition programs serve two preventive functions: education, and early detection of health problems. Other preventive services include screening programs for high blood pressure, glaucoma, hearing, chest disorders, diabetes, etc. Accessible locales and communication of availability should be standards guiding community placement of services.

Home health care services should receive additional support as they are directed to older women. Studies consistently show that those ill older persons who receive appropriate services within their own homes are able to maintain their independence. Present interest in these services emphasizes the concept of minimal intervention. Home care programs designed for minimal intervention can be coordinated and sponsored by a variety of agencies, and are particularly useful for those elderly with emotional or mental handicaps. Suggested home service providers include visiting nurses, mutual help groups, physician assistants, and part-time household workers. These service providers can spend a minimal amount of time attending to the elderly person's needs, yet enable the elderly to remain independent. For example, visiting nurses can check on or give medications, neighborhood help groups can check daily by phone to assure the elderly person's well-being, household workers can help ill persons dress, bathe, cook, and clean. Along with the services that home health workers can provide, they can act as a social contact with the outside world to help reduce isolationism. Hence, the variety of health problems necessitates a responding spectrum of acute, chronic, and preventive services aimed at maximizing enjoyment of the expanding life cycle of females.

EDUCATION PROGRAMS

Education programs can facilitate the many mid and late life adjustments for women. Three essential educational subjects that can remedy both immediate and extended circumstances are financial management, career skills, and driver training. Services which are designed both to teach and assist in personal financial management would give the older woman confidence in her own ability. A major topic should be general management of the home and other assets. Other topics include whether to maintain or sell a home which is beyond the needs of the occupant and techniques to make a home more energy-efficient. Moreover, financial management education should attempt to alert the women to fraudulent schemes, especially those of insurance policies and home repair. A second essential education program, that of employment skills preparation, can give women the opportunity either to renew previous skills or attain capabilities for a second career. Driver training is the third suggested essential education program. Driving skills increase the ability to access services. Many women have unused automobiles and are reluctant to drive, maintaining the belief that driving was a responsibility of the husband. Thus, many women became totally dependent for mobility. This immobility may stimulate feelings of helplessness and strain family/friend relationships. Changing situations and specially designed courses can provide the opportunity for a new found independence.

OUTREACH PROGRAMS

The purpose of outreach is to increase accessibility to services. Outreach services should provide older women with information about and linkage to available services. Since many older women are unaware of programs designed to meet their needs or reluctant to assert themselves, outreach should have three facets. The first is the identification and location of potential clients. This has been discussed earlier as a crucial client/service obstacle. The second facet of outreach is information and referral which further matches relief to need. The third aspect of outreach is the transportation component. People in need can only avail themselves of services if they can reach them. To offer services to elderly without corollary transportation units negates program design.

INCOME PROGRAMS

It is acknowledged that state and local programs designed for women are not able to address the major problem of inadequate income. Changes are most probable from national level legislation. However, there are several strategies that could produce beneficial results. Women are second class citizens regarding Social Security benefits. They are the primary recipients of Social Security but are blocked from economic security because of discriminatory and unequal treatment. Four major areas in Social Security reform should be addressed by females and aging advocacy groups: 1) restrictive benefits—women who work must be allowed to collect their benefits as both worker and wife; 2) widow's benefits—widowed women under age sixty-two, with adult children, must be allowed to collect Social Security; 3) interrupted work patterns—there must be an adjustment when computing benefits for women who choose to interrupt careers for the motherhood years; 4) housewife benefits—no woman should be penalized because she chooses to work in the home instead of in the labor force. A second strategy to attain a more adequate income is through expanded community-based training and employment services for older females exemplified by the successful displaced homemakers programs.

RESPITE CARE

Respite care is a necessary element of any service program for the elderly. Respite services are those provided so that individuals who must care for the ill elderly on a 24-hour basis may have short relief periods. Respite services can be provided for short time spans by trained day or night sitters or for longer periods. Family members or nonrelated care providers can then have the opportunity to enjoy their own activities. The knowledge that one can be temporarily relieved has been more important to care providers than the program itself. This service can be most significant for both wives of ill men and families of advanced-age females. The first group needs to protect their own well-being as providers and the latter group requires a restive focus to diffuse their own potentially abusive behavior.

Providers

The third major issue cluster to be addressed deals with concerns about the potential deliverers or providers of services to the female portion of the aging population. The concerns include a delineation of: who might be the appropriate providers; the apparent trends in planning service provision; and requirements in the nurturing of probable service providers.

The range of potential service providers to older women can be conceptualized in a twofold classification: formal and informal. The formal grouping represents systematic, organized, and community level service delivery mechanisms. The formal class could include community volunteers, private-pay agency personnel, and governmental agency personnel. The informal group represents less sytematic and organized approaches in responding to human need. The informal class could be comprised of adult child, other relative, or friend/neighbor.

The array of appropriate potential providers suggests that program designers take into account some emerging trends when planning service provision. One such trend is the increasing acceptability of formal networks as service providers. The younger segment of the aging female population is more accustomed to interacting with government agencies and private firms in many aspects of their lives. Hence, an implication is that they would not have to know a person previously in order to relate to them in a client/service circumstance.

A second emerging trend that could effect the development of providers is the legal responsibility of the child for the parent. This legislative trend is spreading across various states. Over the years, government programs have been replacing the informal support system of the family. The implication for program planners is to build service packages that work to strengthen and not replace the family. Legal responsibility for parents should be encouraged and formal support services should supplement and complement existing informal support relationships.

A final significant phenomenon that merits recognition in the development of appropriate providers is social bonding. One of the crucial problems of old age is isolation. As friends and family within the elderly person's age group begin to die, social ties are reduced. Retirement further reduces outside contacts. Weakening kinship ties, as younger family members grow away from older members, further isolates the old. Social bonding, whether derived from work, family, or peer relationships, is important for each person if that person is to maintain a healthy outlook on life. When elderly women live in community settings, i.e., the same apartment building, a form of social bonding known as sibling bonding, may occur. Elderly female friends and neighbors take on a kinship role. Bonding promotes communal solidarity which prevents the feeling of social isolation. Widows can take comfort from other women who take a "family" interest in their welfare. The acceptance of bonding and the foster of mutual-help systems should be encouraged by programs which utilize women as direct providers to each other.

A major problem with service provisions to older women is the mixture of a lack of expertise and a negative bias about this population segment on the part of professional practitioners. Thus, the final concern for program planners involves the requirement of nurturing providers who will be sensitive and aware of older women. This nurturing and grooming of providers can be achieved through staff education. Attitudes and stereotypes held about the elderly are difficult to change. Since these attitudes directly affect the quality of service provision, special emphasis should be made to change them. Attitudinal surveys have shown the need for training in gerontology, particularly for health workers. The biased health or social service worker may wonder if services to the elderly are truly needed since the end of life is near. Educating workers to accept the idea that old age can be a productive period of life will bring beneficial results to clients.

CONCLUSION

This chapter addressed the needs of elderly women within the context of their unique differences from the general population of elderly. The major focus has been on the identification of this group as a target population, the initial services which should be provided for older women, and the delineation of service providers. As program planners and policy makers look to a future population of active, elderly women, they must design programs which allow these women to maintain their independence and make viable contributions to our world.

REFERENCES

Binstock, R.H., & Shanas, E. (Eds.). *Handbook of Aging and the Social Sciences.* New York: Van Nostrand Reinhold Company, 1976.

Brody, J.E. Menopausal Estrogens: Benefits and Risks of the "Feminine" Drug. *Forum,* National Action Forum for Older Women, Rockville, Maryland: National Institute of Mental Health, Vol. 2, no. 2, Fall 1979.

Burkhauser, R.V. Are Women Treated Fairly in Today's Social Security System? *The Gerontologist,* 1979, *19*:3, 242–249.

Dancy, J., Jr. *The Black Elderly: A Guide for Practitioners,* The University of Michigan-Wayne State University: The Institute of Gerontology, 1977.

Davis, L.J., & Brody, E.M. *Rape and Older Women: A Guide to Prevention and Protection.* Rockville, Maryland: National Institute of Mental Health, 1979.

Fengler, A.P., & Goodrich, N. Wives of Elderly Disable Men: The Hidden Patients. *The Gerontologist,* 1979, *19*:2, 175–183.

Hochschild, A.R. *The Unexpected Community: Portrait of An Old Age Subculture.* Berkeley: University of California Press, 1978.

Hollenshead, C.H., Katz, C., & Ingersoll, B. *Past Sixty: The Older Woman in Print and Film.* The University of Michigan-Wayne State University, Institute of Gerontology, 1977.

Holtzman, J.M., Beck, J.D., & Ettinger, R.I. Cognitive Knowledge and Attitudes Toward the Aged of Dental and Medical Students. *Educational Gerontology, 1981, Vol. 6, 196-207.*

National Institute on Aging. The Older Woman: Continuities and Discontinuities. Report of the National Institute on Aging and the National Institute of Mental Health Workshop. Washington, D.C.: U.S. Government Printing Office, 1979.

Seltzer, M.M., Corbett, S.L., & Atchley, R.C. *Social Problems of the Aging: Readings.* Belmont, California, Wadsworth Publishing Co., Inc., 1978.

Smith, B.K. *The Pursuit of Dignity: New Living Alternatives for the Elderly.* Boston: Beacon Press, 1977.

Tobin, S.S., Davidson, S.M., & Sack, A. *Effective Social Services for Older Americans.* The University of Michigan-Wayne State University, Institute of Gerontology, 1976.

Women in Crisis: Centers Sometimes Make the Difference. *Aging,* nos. 283–284, 1978, 16–17.

INDEX